Bert Bielefeld

Climate-Smart Design and Construction

BAS

Bert Bielefeld

Climate-Smart Design and Construction

BIRKHÄUSER
BASEL

Contents

Foreword

Exponential progress over the last 100 years has revolutionized people's way of life and their raison d'être, even though this progress has not yet reached everyone. The drive for growth and improvement has a number of far-reaching advantages, but also one very significant disadvantage: it relies on the use of fossil and mineral resources, the consumption of which more often than not exacts a heavy price on nature and the climate. For many decades, people in the so-called "industrialized nation" have lived beyond their means, with the result that the complicated mechanisms governing the climate and ecosystems are undergoing rapid change. In order to prevent the collapse of many systems and to avoid jeopardizing human development it is imperative for us to radically reduce behaviors that damage the environment and to find ways – as quickly as possible – of reestablishing our standards of living based on climate neutrality.

The construction and operation of buildings is an important element in this process of transformation because a significant proportion of the world's greenhouse gases are produced in the construction sector. For this reason, a paradigm shift is needed in how buildings are designed, constructed, and used. In order to consider key principles from the very beginning, it is necessary to fully understand all options available in climate-sensitive design and construction. In addition to technical solutions, this means a deep understanding of how design decisions impact the final outcome. It is important to treat climate concerns as an integral element of the design task and to look for creative solutions beyond the conventional. *Climate-Smart Design and Construction* offers a comprehensive introduction and helps readers develop their own creative approaches and strategies.

Bert Bielefeld
Editor

Introduction

The world's resources are being used up at a frightening pace. This simple statement reflects the progressive overexploitation of natural resources over two centuries of industrialization, leading to anthropogenic or man-made climate change. Climate change will alter many existing structures, even leading in part to the destruction of the earth's climate, ecosystems, weather systems, basic food supplies, and ultimately our entire way of life. For this reason, all of humanity – and in particular the populations of affluent nations – must engage in a transformation process that needs to start immediately. Specifically, we must decarbonize key sectors of the economy in order to mitigate the effects of climate change.

A key sector in this context is the construction industry and, generally, the operation of buildings, because this sector accounts for 40 to 50 percent of worldwide CO_2 emissions. A paradigm shift in construction, building conversion, and the use and operation of buildings can be a key driver of climate protection alongside general consumption, manufacturing industries, and transportation. This requires an enormous effort and fundamental questioning of many established habits and structures. "Business as usual" is no longer a viable option.

It is important to note that the objective cannot be achieved with one single concept. Rather, it is necessary to make use of various approaches in order to reduce greenhouse gas emissions and resource consumption as much as possible. Moreover, this must be considered during the design

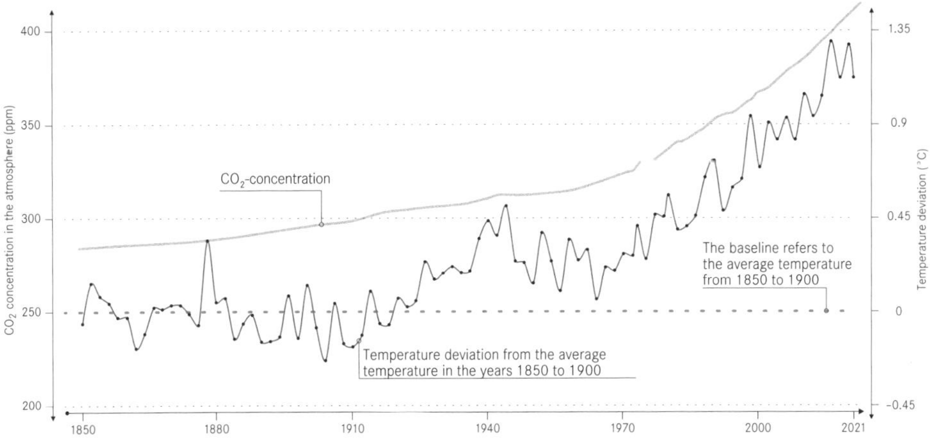

Fig. 1: Relationship between CO_2 concentration and deviations of average temperature from the long-term baseline

process, starting with the definition of framework conditions and continuing through to completion.

In the chapters below, we will cover a range of aspects and approaches. After explaining the basic issues related to climate change, we will look at the emissions and energy consumption of buildings. Taking into account the lifecycle of new and existing buildings, we will then consider the basis for various instruments and strategies for climate-sensitive construction. Finally, we will consider the process, describing all design stages – from development of the brief through to implementation – of climate-appropriate design and construction.

Climate change

FACTORS IMPACTING THE CLIMATE

Our climate is determined by the solar radiation that reaches the earth. In part, solar radiation is reflected back into space by the water vapor in clouds, by various gases in the air, and by the earth's surface. In order to achieve a balanced climate on earth, the amount of solar radiation that is retained in the atmosphere must be equal that of the overall loss of radiated heat from the earth. If this equation is no longer equal, the earth's heat balance changes, upsetting its highly complex climate systems. ○

Earth's atmosphere

In addition to cyclical adaptations such as variations in solar radiation and changes in the earth's orbit around the sun, mankind has been increasingly disturbing the balance in radiation since industrialization. The composition of our atmosphere has changed largely due to the increase in the burning of fossil fuels for energy over the last 100 years, resulting in an increasing accumulation of greenhouse gases. We have seen a rapid increase in the net emissions of greenhouse gases such as carbon dioxide and methane, especially over the last 30 years > Fig. 2. Greenhouse gases reduce the amount of heat radiated into space, reflecting it back to earth instead, which is why the earth is becoming steadily warmer.

Tipping points

Some of the systems that are important for maintaining the global climatic balance initially remain stable. However, as soon as a tipping point is reached, they quickly become unstable or shift entirely. This can lead to sustained and irreparable changes in the climate system. Examples of tipping points include the loss of ice caps at the South and North Poles, ocean current circulation, the melting of boreal permafrost soils, worldwide coral die-off, the loss of mountain glaciers, and extensive changes in vegetation, such as in the Amazon rainforest. ●

○ **Note**: Long-term and supra-regional climate data cannot be compared with local weather phenomena or variations in weather patterns. Climate research deals with changes over long periods of at least 30 years and uses measurement data to establish statistical evaluations and prognoses. Changes in certain regions or over periods of time, as well as extreme events, can be caused by changes in the world's complex climate systems but can also be based on normal variations in the weather.

● **Example**: Global warming causes melting in the polar regions and successive thawing of permafrost soils. This releases greenhouse gases that are currently trapped there and, in addition, accelerates global warming. At the same time, it is possible for cold zones to arise, for example when the Gulf Stream decreases in strength and eventually no longer delivers sufficient heat to Europe. This causes many systems to become imbalanced, which can have a variety of consequences.

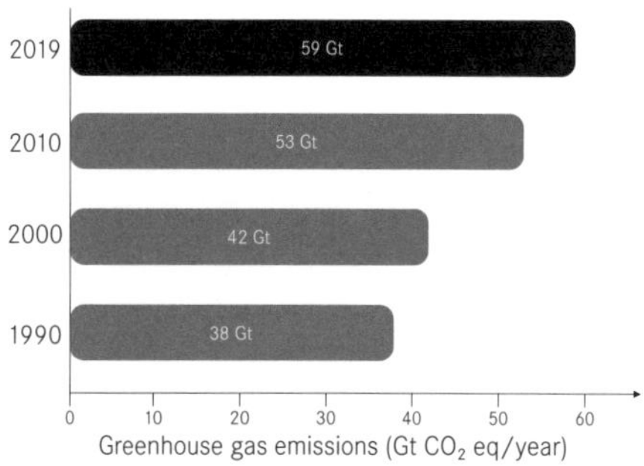

Fig. 2: Trend of annual greenhouse gas emissions over the last 30 years

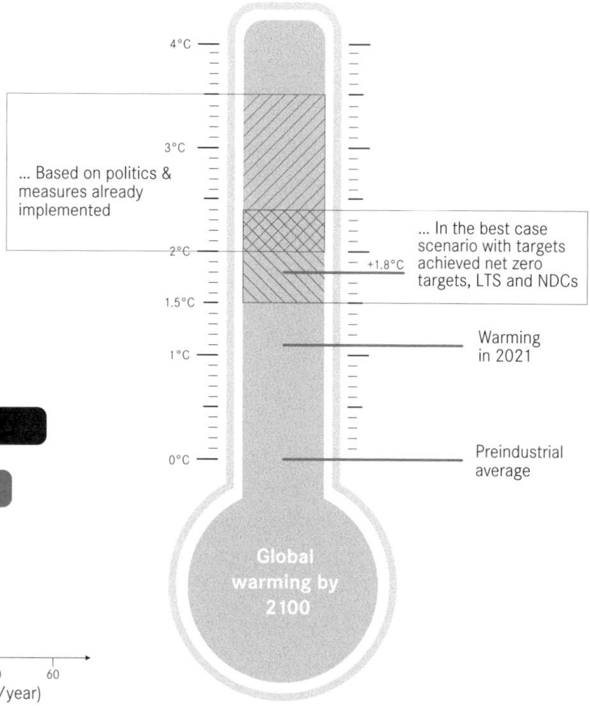

Fig. 3: Possible extent of global warming

Limiting global temperature change to 1.5 °C

At the 2015 UN Climate Conference in Paris, it was decided to try to limit global warming to a maximum of 1.5 °C. By now, this objective seems unrealistic for almost all nations owing to the lack of effective measures taken. However, global warming by even 2 °C is expected to generate environmental crises. These include significantly more frequent and severe extreme weather events such as heatwaves and flooding, mass extinctions on land and in the ocean, difficulties for agriculture, major increases in sea levels, as well as the loss of habitable regions and the resulting climate migration > Fig. 3.

KEY TARGETS

Through the UN climate conferences that are held at regular intervals, the global community of nations is endeavoring to reach consensus as to how to limit global warming. The negotiating processes are complex and lengthy because a wide range of interests and needs have to be synchronized and the social buffering required by the necessary

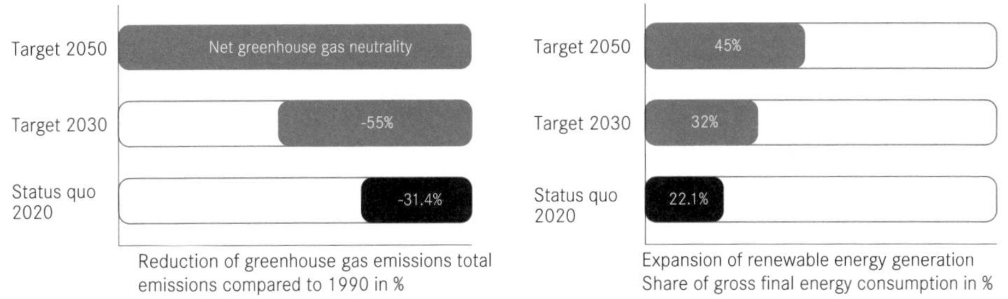

Fig. 4: Climate targets of the European Union

transformation processes affect different nations and regions differently.

Most industrial nations have set targets that are intended to strike a balance between the urgently needed paradigm shift and the consequences for their national economies. For example, the European Union wants to reduce its greenhouse gas emissions by 55 percent from the 1990 baseline by 2030 and to be greenhouse-gas neutral by 2050 > Fig. 4. Such targets and implementation strategies are subject to regular negotiations and modifications, because the necessary change processes have a major impact in many private, social, and economic spheres.

It is crucial that nations with very high greenhouse gas emissions agree on binding reduction targets and that nations that are in an earlier development phase or already face serious climate-change consequences receive appropriate support. Historically, the regions with the highest greenhouse gas emissions are North America and Europe. Over the last three decades, East Asia has contributed a significant proportion to greenhouse gas emissions owing to strong economic development > Fig. 5. However, in terms of emissions per capita, North America is still number one > Fig. 6.

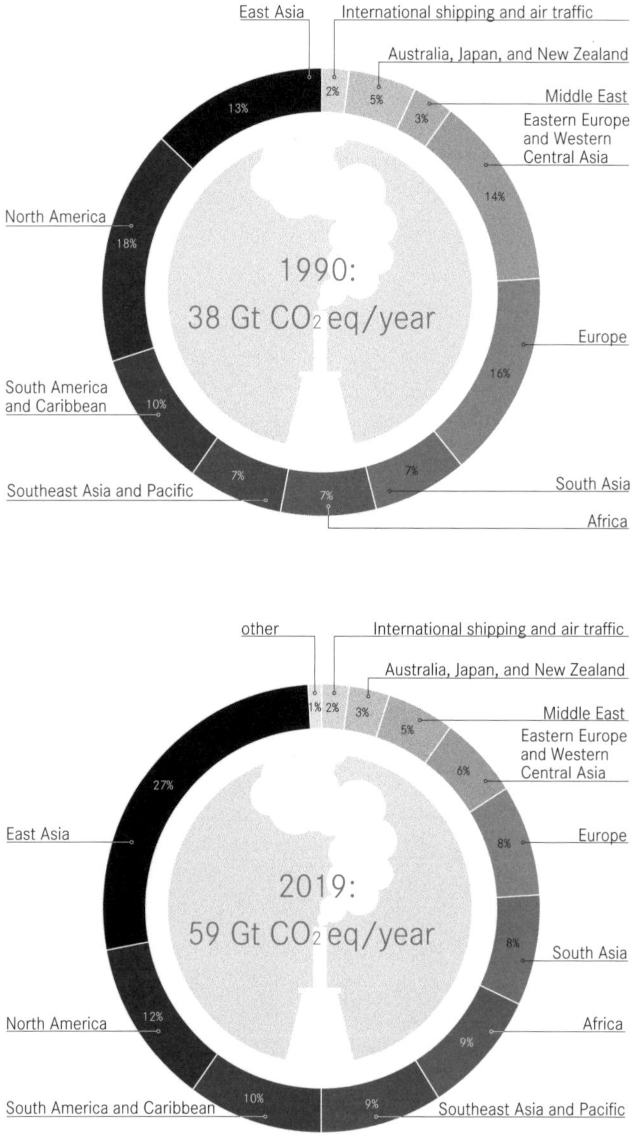

Fig. 5: World regions and their contribution to global greenhouse gas emissions

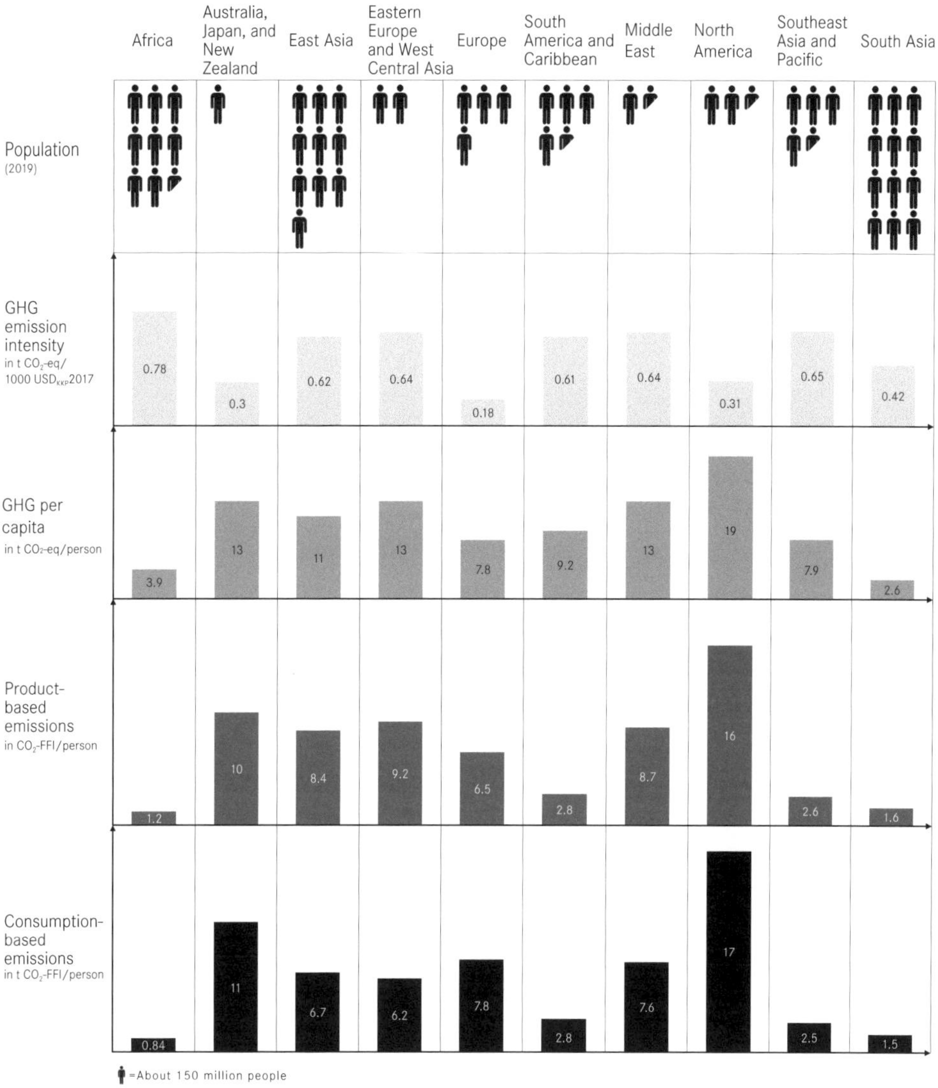

Fig. 6: Global greenhouse gas emissions per capita

TRANSFORMATION TO CLIMATE NEUTRALITY

When the Club of Rome published *The Limits to Growth* in 1972, providing for the first time scientific evidence that our planet's resources are finite and that the limits of resource use would soon be reached, this stimulated a broad scientific discourse. Unfortunately, this has not led to any tangible change in the way the planet's resources are managed, which means that – in many areas – we have already exceeded the limit of resources and irreparable damage has been done > Fig. 7.

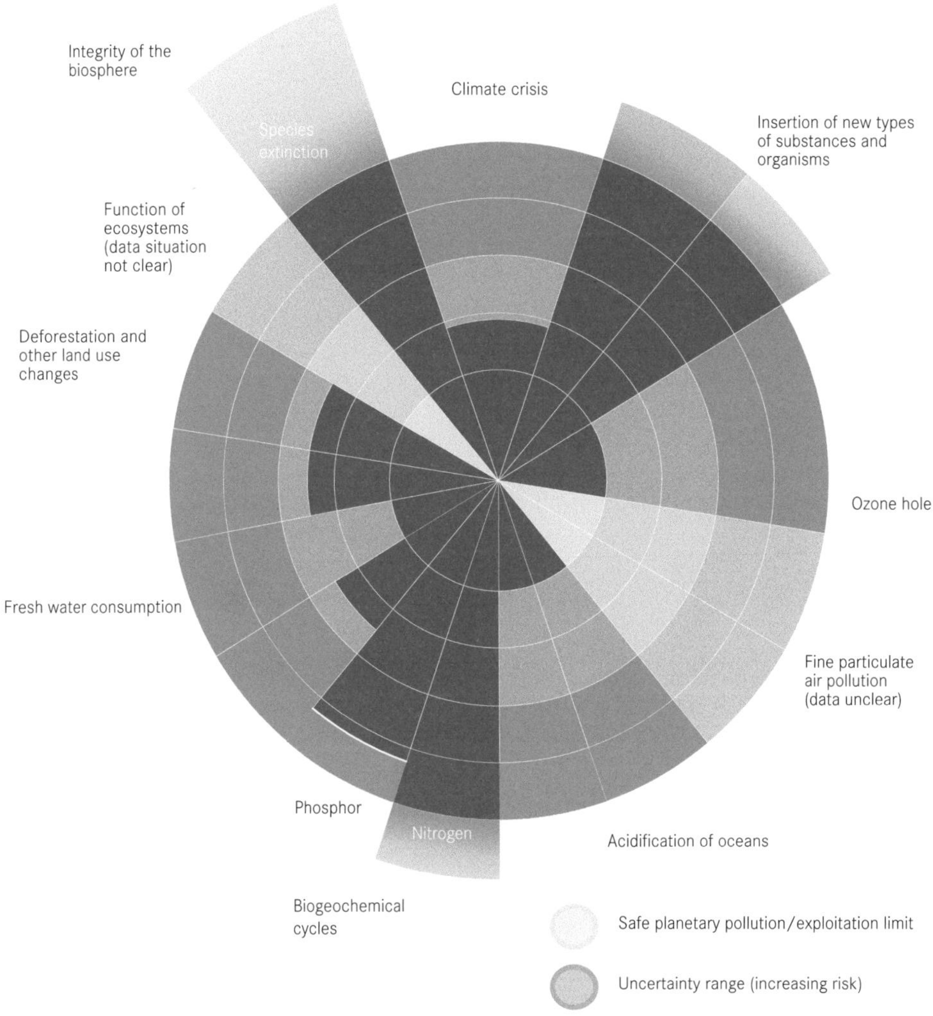

Fig. 7: The earth's ecological limits in terms of pollution/resource exploitation

Climate neutrality

Nevertheless, it must be the primary objective of all efforts – though this may initially appear utopian – to compensate for changes that have already taken place and halt the process of climate change so that important tipping points are not reached. It is imperative, at a minimum, that all industries, nations, and societies work towards climate neutrality as urgently as possible so that no further finite resources are consumed.

Social sustainability

Climate-friendly transformation of economies must go hand-in-hand with social sustainability, as defined by the United Nations > Fig. 8. Because without simultaneous improvement of the living conditions of all people who, already now, strongly feel the effects of climate change, and without a needs-adjusted foundation for all people globally, such complex and far-reaching transformation processes cannot be implemented. ■

Fig. 8: The United Nations' Sustainable Development Goals (SDGs)

○ **Note**: The Club of Rome is an informal non-profit organization of scientists from all over the world, headquartered in Switzerland. As a follow-up to *The Limits to Growth, the Club published Earth for All* in 2022, which summarizes complex development prognoses to offer a view of the future of our planet.

■ **Tip**: Kate Raworth, a British scientist based at the University of Oxford, has developed a model of "doughnut economics", which balances planetary and social limits (see Fig. 9). It establishes a new point of emphasis in the evaluation of economics, thus marking a shift away from compulsive growth.

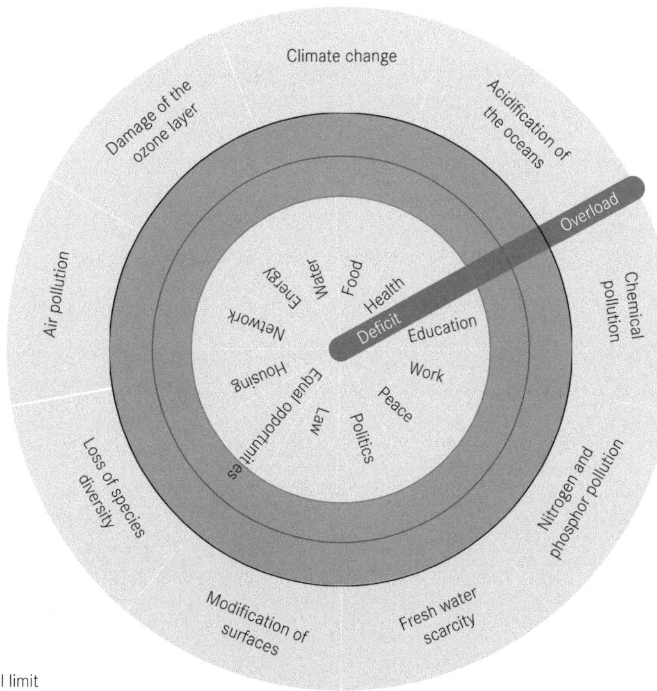

Fig. 9: "Doughnut economics", an economic model developed by Kate Raworth

THE RISK OF GLOBAL WARMING

The most essential factor in global warming is the greenhouse effect. The most relevant greenhouse gas in terms of atmospheric heat retention is water vapor, which has always played the decisive role in the natural balance of the atmosphere. In second place is carbon dioxide (CO_2), whose concentration has increased from about 280 ppm (parts per million) in the preindustrial era to over 400 ppm due to anthropogenic emissions. Though there are many other gases that contribute to the greenhouse effect and are much more damaging than an equal amount of CO_2, CO_2 is the most significant greenhouse gas owing to the large proportion of emissions (over 80 percent).

Global warming potential (GWP)

Because many gases occur in significantly smaller volumes and it was necessary to take into account different factors and gases, conversion factors were established for these other gases. These are used to

Fig. 10: CO_2 equivalent of important greenhouse gases. Source: IPCC 5th Assessment Report, 2014

Greenhouse gas		Life span in the atmosphere	GWP (for period of 20 years)	GWP (for period of 100 years)	GTP (for period of 20 years)	GTP (for period of 100 years)
Carbon dioxide	CO_2	varies	1	1	1	1
Methane	CH_4	12.4 years	84	28	67	4
Dinitrogen oxide	N_2O	121 years	264	265	277	234
Tetrafluoromethane	CF_4	50,000 years	4880	6630	5270	8040

calculate their global warming potential in comparable terms to CO_2. This variable, which is known as "CO_2 equivalent" or "global warming potential (GWP)", includes all major greenhouse gases converted to the equivalent effect of CO_2 over a specific time period > Fig. 10. The time period is relevant because these gases remain in the atmosphere for different periods of time and hence their effects vary in duration.

○ Other potentials

In addition to the global warming potential (GWP), these gases affect other systems, and these other negative potentials should be taken into account in mitigation planning. These include, for example,

- the ozone depletion potential (ODP), e.g. from fluoro-chlorinated hydrocarbons, which damage the protective ozone layer;
- the acidification potential (AP), e.g. from sulfur dioxide, which can damage ecosystems in the form of acid rain;
- the eutrophication potential (EP), e.g. caused by phosphates and nitrates, which can damage ecosystems; and
- the photochemical ozone creation potential (POCP), e.g. caused by nitrogen oxide, which can lead to smog in the lower atmospheric layers.

○ **Note**: Global warming potential (GWP) covers the sum of all climate effects for the time period under consideration, whereas the global temperature potential (GTP) is a variable for the actual temperature change at the end of the time period under consideration.

Resource and energy consumption

In order to promote transformation processes, we must consider and minimize these potentials, in particular CO_2 equivalent, in the lifecycle of buildings. This means taking into account the resources needed from construction through to operation and conversion, or change of use, and finally disposal. In the context of buildings, this means locally used resources, building and auxiliary materials, as well as the energy used during the lifecycle, for example for heating and cooling.

ENERGY AND RESOURCE CONSUMPTION IN BUILDINGS

Resource consumption as part of construction

The construction of a building requires an immense mass of materials, which in turn requires an enormous investment of energy, both to produce the materials and to use them on site. Very few building materials can be produced without gray energy (energy produced from polluting sources) or CO_2 emissions, which means that the enormous mass involved in the new building will always involve a high CO_2 equivalent output.

It is not always easy to ascertain which resources, and how many of them, are used in a building material > Fig. 12. Because manufacturers use different production methods and there is a growing focus on climate-smart

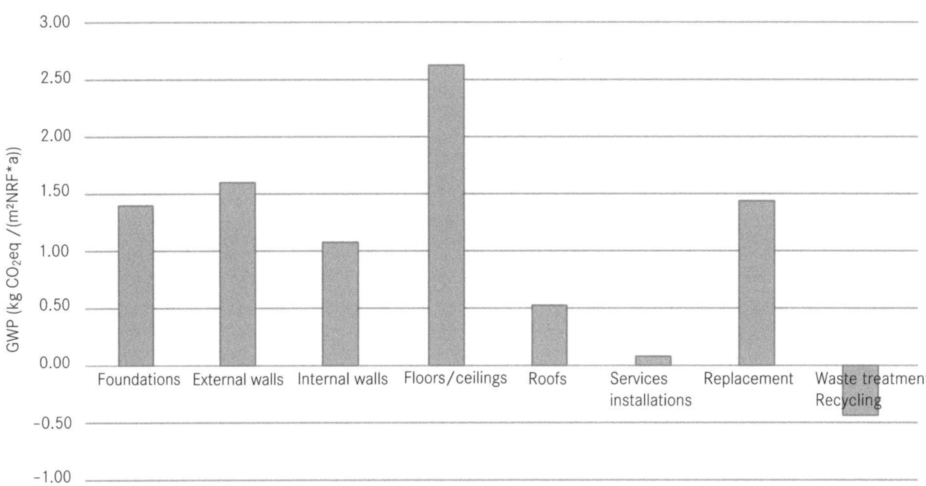

Fig. 11: Example of the material resources used in a new building

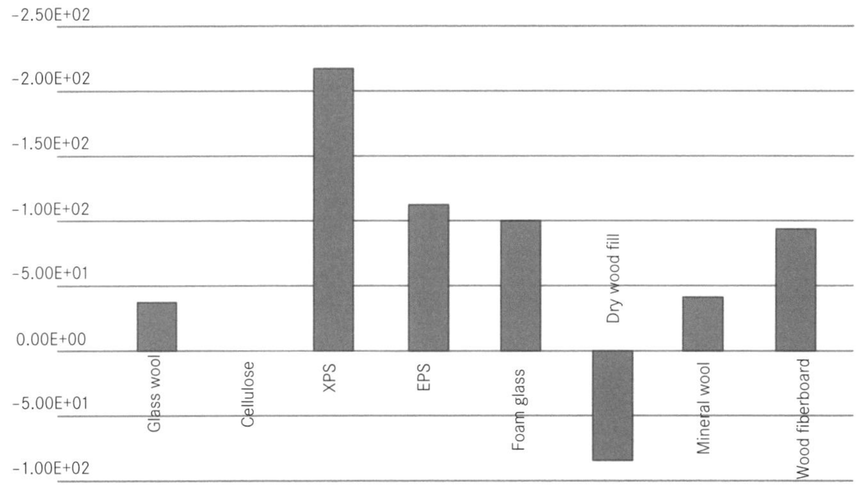

Fig. 12: Example of resources used in the production of different insulation materials (production, construction, and disposal phases in accordance with DIN EN 15804)

production, there can be significant variation in how much energy and other resources are used to produce each type of building material.

Energy consumption in operation

Even though the input of resources and energy during the construction of a building is immense, this still represents just 20 to 25 percent of the total input during the building's entire lifecycle, depending on service life. During a long service life, energy consumption adds up considerably - especially in the case of poorly insulated buildings.

Heat generation

In temperate and colder regions, an important part in the operation of a building is the generation of heat. The production of heat using fossil fuels such as oil, gas, or coal produces high CO_2 emissions, which can only be reduced through efficiency measures such as optimized thermal insulation and minimized heat losses. It makes more sense to generate heat from regenerative sources such as geothermal or solar

■ **Tip**: Since the majority of resources are used to construct the shell, envelope and fit-out, it is generally best - for the sake of climate-smart construction - to make use of any existing building fabric (see chapter on Climate-Smart Strategies).

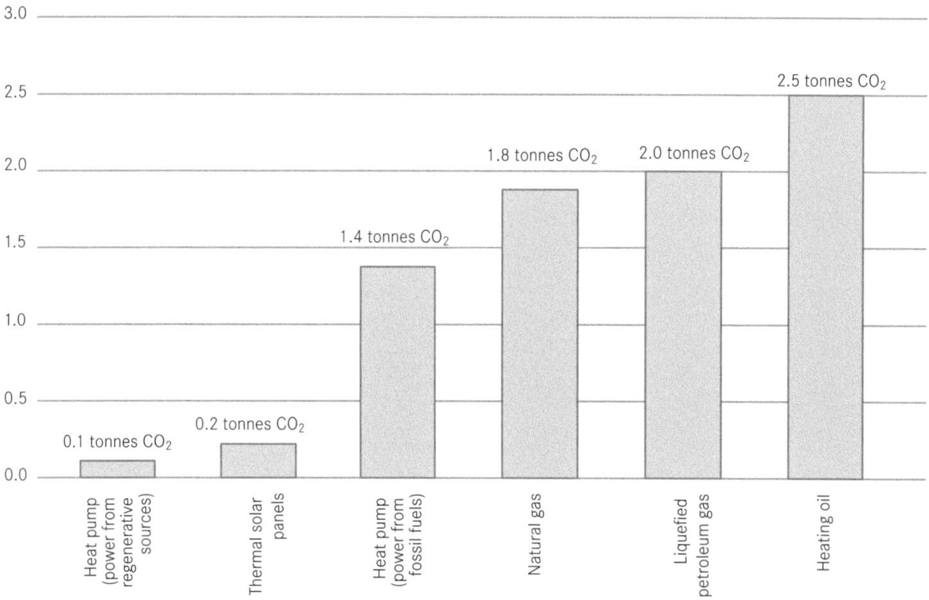

CO_2 emissions for different types of heating systems; annual consumption for 4-person household in a 200 sqm apartment building

Fig. 13: CO_2 emissions for different energy sources used to heat buildings

energy, although it is important to note that such systems usually consume quite a significant amount of electricity. This electricity consumption must also be covered from regenerative sources in order to avoid the indirect use of gray energy. This may result in complex installations ○ > Fig. 13.

Cooling generation

Buildings that are well insulated may experience net heat gain due to the heat generated by human occupants or technical installations such as monitors and computers, and they cannot compensate for this heat gain through natural ventilation. Such buildings have to be cooled. Moreover, in warm and humid climate zones, air-conditioning is often needed to ensure comfortable ambient temperatures. Cooling and air-conditioning systems - particularly if used to regulate humidity - consume a lot of energy. For this reason, it is advisable, where possible, to avoid the installation of a classic cooling/air-conditioning system. It is often possible to significantly reduce the need for cooling by using designs that are ● adapted to local climatic conditions.

However, certain functional buildings, such as museums and research establishments, require a specific standard internal climate. In such cases, technical installations are usually necessary.

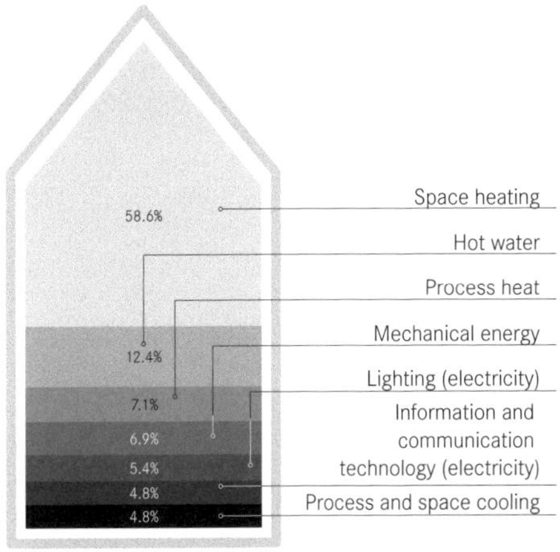

Fig. 14: Final energy consumption during the operational life of a building

Power consumption

During the usage phase of a building, attention must be paid to power consumption. This includes fixed installations such as lighting systems, which can be controlled using LED technology, and automatic controls such as movement or light sensors. The electricity consumption of technical equipment such as computers must also be taken into consideration. These should consume as little energy as possible.

Maintenance and repair

It is also necessary to take into account the energy used to maintain and repair building components, surfaces, and installations. Considering the resources invested in construction, one should aim for the longest possible service life. This helps to defray the loss represented by resource use. In order to ensure a long service life, many building components and installations may require regular servicing and maintenance, as well

○ **Note**: Where it is intended to heat a building entirely from regenerative sources, the question arises whether to use the highest possible standard of insulation. This is important because the production of the most frequently used insulating materials also requires much gray energy. A solution may be to insulate a building only to the extent that the chosen method of heating functions well and the necessary comfort levels are achieved inside the building. Over the lifecycle of a building, this minimizes CO_2 output and the consumption of gray energy.

● **Example**: It is possible to reduce the heat gain through the use of construction elements that provide shade and to compensate for internally generated heat using other measures, such as an ice store, thermal mass activation, or night cooling. These use significantly less energy than a technical installation using cooling aggregates.

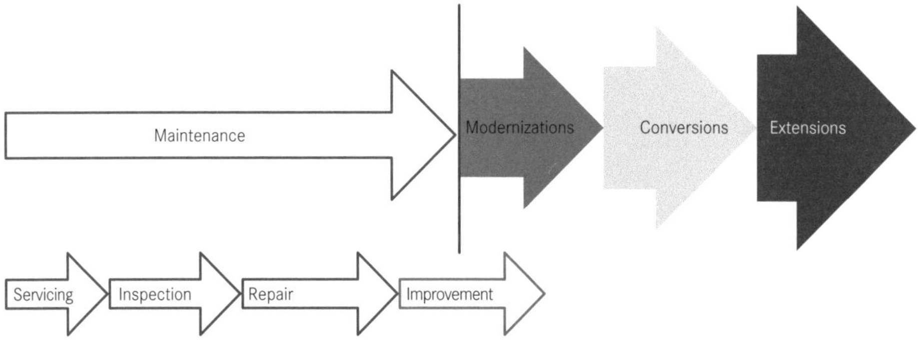

Fig. 15: Stages involved in the maintenance and repair of existing buildings

as repair where appropriate > Fig. 15. These measures consume significantly fewer resources than frequent replacement of components and installations.

For the construction and operational measures described above, the energy used is key to climate protection, because the focus is not only on material resources but also on the energy consumed in production. For this reason, a distinction needs to be made below between different sources of energy.

PRIMARY ENERGY

Often, buildings are evaluated and categorized based on their demand for primary energy. Primary energy refers to energy embedded in the different fuels that have not yet been processed. Examples of primary energy sources are crude fossil fuels (i.e. coal, natural gas, petroleum oil), nuclear energy, and regenerative sources such as wind, water, and solar energy. Part of the primary energy is lost in conversion to secondary energy, such as electricity or combustion fuels. The energy used by the consumer is referred to as final energy.

Primary energy requirement

In the context of a national economy as well as an individual building, the primary energy requirement takes into account all processes and production and transport losses > Fig. 16. The primary energy requirement is therefore an important factor in assessing the ecological balance of a building.

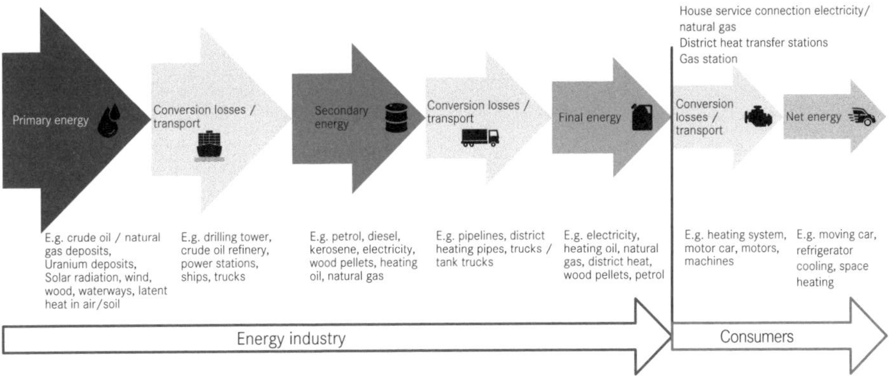

Fig. 16: Production chain of primary energy, secondary energy, and final energy

GRAY ENERGY

In order to accurately determine resource consumption in buildings, it is important to consider gray energy. Gray energy (measured in kilowatt hours or in megajoules) refers to the total energy "embodied" in building materials as a result of the extraction of raw materials, as well as the production, sale, transport, installation, and disposal of a material. This calculation is complex because many different components must be taken into account, and results vary due to the production of identical products at different sites.

Gray energy expenditure is not equivalent to CO_2 emissions, because it is possible to produce the required energy in a climate-neutral way.

About 80 percent of the gray energy used in construction is embodied in the shell and building envelope. For this reason, it is nearly always more energy-efficient to refurbish or redevelop existing buildings. > Chapter Climate-Smart Strategies

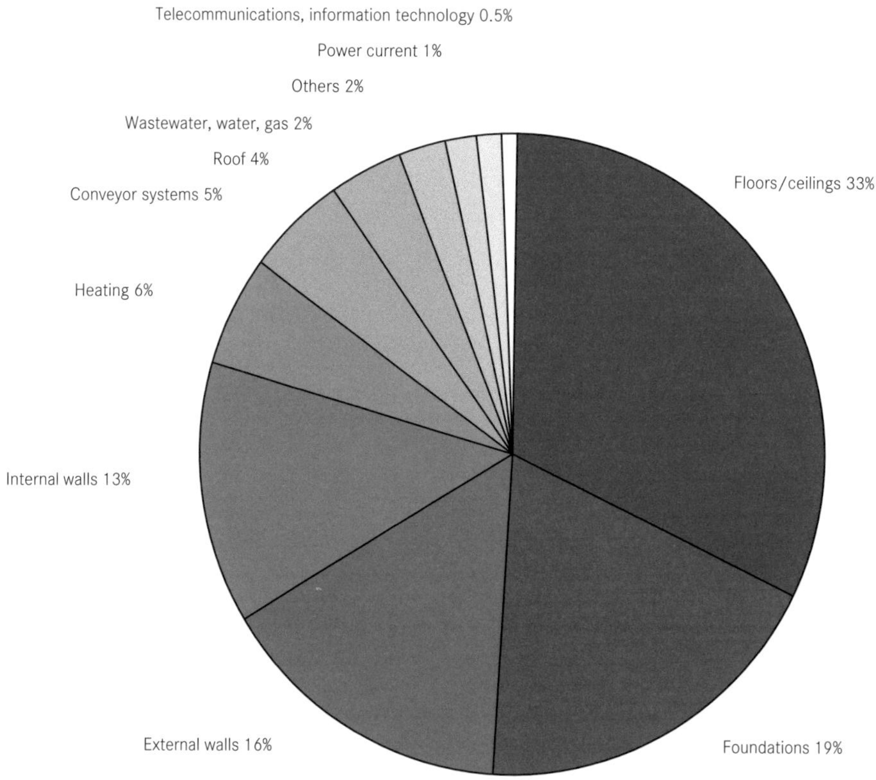

Fig. 17: Gray energy expenditure of an apartment building over an 80-year service life

FOSSIL AND RENEWABLE ENERGY

A further important distinction is that between fossil and renewable energies.

Fossil energy

Fossil energy is extracted from hydrocarbon fuels such as crude oil, natural gas, black coal, and brown coal, or peat, which consist of decomposed plant and animal matter from the geological past. Even though some of these still exist in large deposits, they are nevertheless considered finite resources because they take millions of years to form. During fossil fuel combustion, carbon combines with oxygen in air to form carbon dioxide (CO_2), the key driver of the greenhouse effect.

Biomass/wood

Biomass residues from agriculture, as well as wood, are not considered fossil fuels. Even though they release CO_2 during combustion and decomposition, this is less worrisome because they also remove CO_2 from the atmosphere during growth. However, ideally, the embedded greenhouse gases should not be released again, which is why the focus of energy generation should be on renewable energies.

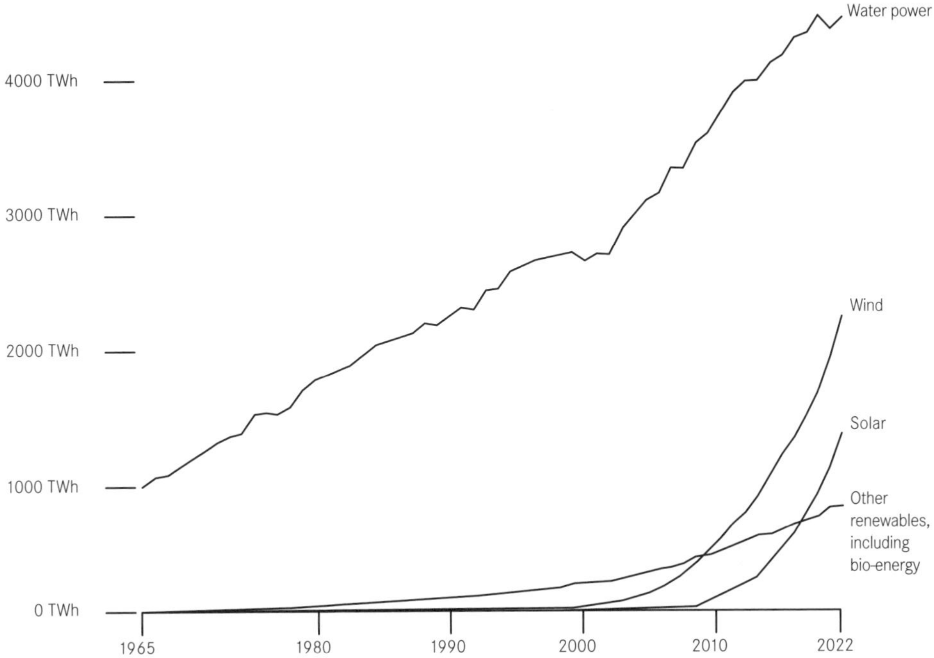

Fig. 18: Global generation of renewable energy

Renewable energy

Renewable energy refers to energy that can be generated in a regenerative manner and, therefore, is available without limit. Examples are:

- Solar energy (for the generation of electricity and heat)
- Hydropower
- Tidal and wave energy
- Wind power
- Geothermal energy

There is a strong worldwide drive to expand the proportion of renewable energy in the energy mix because it is indispensable to achieving the goal of climate neutrality > Fig. 18. Globally, the generation of renewable electricity is now more economical than the burning of fossil fuels, which means that an important milestone has been reached in the transformation process.

Evaluation methods

Various methods exist for assessing the extent to which buildings, products, services, and other processes negatively impact the climate. A few of the most important ones are introduced below.

CO_2 FOOTPRINT / CO_2 BALANCING

The CO_2 footprint, also known as the carbon footprint or CO_2 balancing, evaluates greenhouse gas emissions (global warming potential (GWP)), using carbon dioxide (CO_2) as the important element as the basis for the calculation. In the case of other greenhouse gases such as methane (CH_4) and nitrous oxide (N_2O) specific factors are used to convert their detrimental effect on the climate into an effect equivalent to that of carbon dioxide. > Chapter Climate Change/The Risk of Global Warming

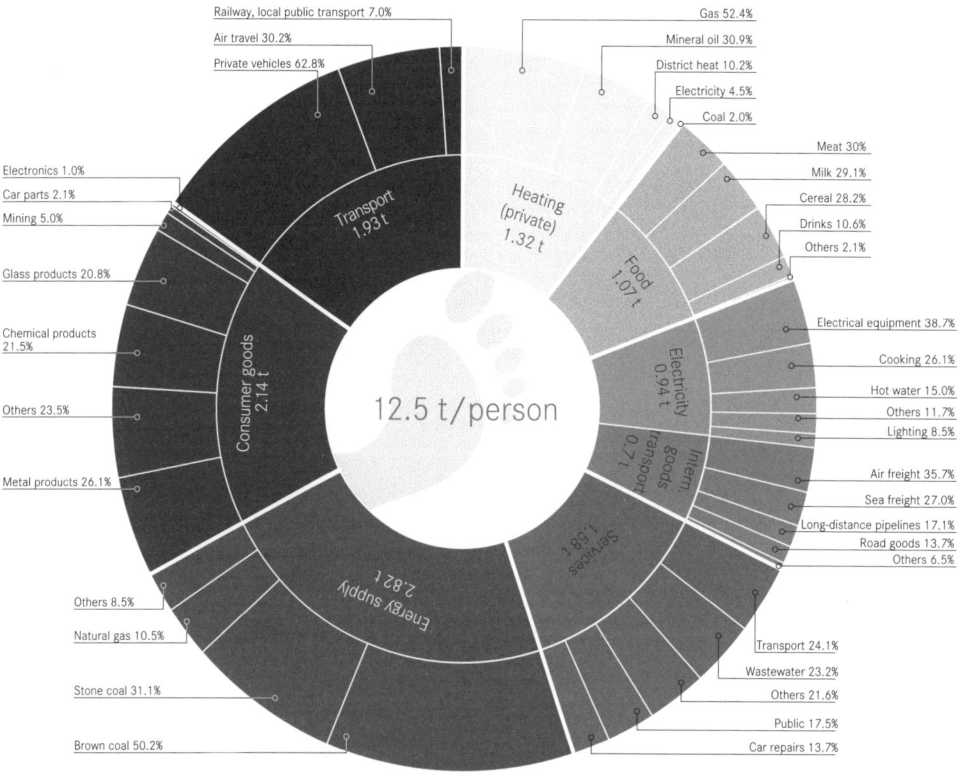

Fig. 19: CO_2 footprint per person in industrial nations

CO_2 footprints are calculated for different contexts. In this way, it is possible to compare the way of life per person in different countries and regions > Fig. 19. Companies also use CO_2 footprints in order to test and document their path towards climate neutrality.

CO_2 balancing for buildings

CO_2 balancing can also be carried out relatively easily for buildings since it only requires the multiplication of the CO_2 equivalents by the existing/planned mass of materials. CO_2 equivalents are provided by manufacturers via so-called environmental product declarations (EPDs) and by independent databases.

ECO-BALANCING AND MATERIAL FLOW ANALYSIS

Eco-balancing

Eco-balancing, which is also referred to as lifecycle assessment (LCA), goes one step further. It is a globally formalized procedure in accordance with ISO 14040/14044. Eco-balancing may be divided into four steps. In the first step, the goal and scope are determined in order to define system limits for data collection and to transparently convey the quality of the data. In the second step, referred to as the lifecycle inventory (LCI), all necessary data on materials, resources, emissions, and waste are compiled in a databank. These are then subjected to a lifecycle impact assessment (LCIA) in the third step. The evaluation carried out in the fourth step relates the result to the defined goals and concludes the eco-balancing process.

Eco-balancing is thus a process that can be used to produce a transparent comparison of the issues under consideration.

Material flow analysis

In contrast to eco-balancing, material flow analysis is not an internationally standardized process, which is why numerous variants exist – some of which are comparable to eco-balancing. In essence, material flow analysis focuses on the flow of substances, materials, and energy associated with a building, a product, a service, or other processes. It, therefore, deals more with the quantities and distances of material flows than with the environmental effects as eco-balancing does.

OTHER EVALUATION METHODS

Below, we provide an overview of a few other approaches that exist in the context of eco-balancing or as statutory regulations.

Lifecycle costing (LCC) uses a similar approach to eco-balancing. However, it focuses primarily on costs, from the design phase via production and use to return. In this way, LCC can integrate climate-related costs and influence decisions on the basis of lifecycle costs.

Social lifecycle assessment (S-LCA)

Social lifecycle assessment (S-LCA) focuses on the social effects of the extraction of raw materials, the manufacture and use of products, and their disposal. It is very similar to eco-balancing but has yet to be uniformly standardized.

Environmental effect assessment

Many nations have developed methods for the assessment of the environmental effects of construction measures, which have to be applied in zoning plans and building applications. The objective is to evaluate any interference with nature, such as soil sealing, so that it can be offset.

EU taxonomy

The European Union, as a large economic entity, uses several different approaches to measuring the environmental impact of construction. In addition to stricter regulations, it has – with the EU taxonomy – established general rules for the definition of sustainable economies, which will have a major influence on the financial system and, hence, on the credit-dependent construction industry.

CERTIFICATION

In addition to the procedures described above, there are also building-related calculation methods that are usually carried out for the purpose of obtaining certification. Such certification requirements are often originally set by individual countries but adopted by others in various forms.

Certification of buildings

Building certifications > Fig. 20 usually contain subcategories that define different sustainability standards for buildings. These are usually associated with complex rules and evaluation criteria, which means that the acquisition of a certificate not only requires compliance with sustainable construction methods but must also consider the cost of monitoring, data processing, and actual certification. Thus, certification can act as an additional evaluation label and increase the value of a property.

Product certification

Certification is available not only for entire buildings but also for individual building products, where it covers different sustainability criteria. There are labels that evaluate a wide range of building products, usually at the national level, and others that cover individual building products, such as timber, or specific criteria, such as interior air quality > Fig. 21.

Fig. 20: Examples of building certification systems

Certificate	Source
LEED	USA
DGNB	Germany
BNB	Germany
BREEAM	United Kingdom
HQE	France
CASBEE	Japan
Green Star	Australia

Fig. 21: Examples of certification systems for building materials

Certificate	Focus	Source
EU Eco-label	Under development, not yet available for all building products	Europe
EPD	Voluntary information provided by manufacturers	Worldwide
Blue Angel	Most types of building products	Germany
Natureplus	Many building products	Germany
FSC	Timber industry	Worldwide
PEFC	Timber industry	Germany, Europe
Green Seal	Many building products	USA
Nordic Swan	Most types of building products	Norway, Sweden, Iceland, Finland, Denmark
Milieukeur	Most types of building products	The Netherlands
Austrian environment label	Many building products	Austria
Cradle to cradle	Circular economy	Worldwide

Climate-smart strategies

Below, we will discuss the instruments and strategies necessary to construct buildings that are as climate-smart as possible and, ideally, climate-neutral. It is important to note that there is no one correct approach. What is needed is a paradigm shift that examines various aspects of the design and construction process. Over the next decade, many approaches will have to be tried and – critically – implemented to identify and establish critical parameters. Contrary to what one might hope, achieving this paradigm shift will not solely rely on innovations, such as market-ready insulation materials derived from regenerative fungi. Furthermore, it is worthwhile to examine the construction methods and principles employed in buildings in sustainably operating cultures to draw relevant conclusions for our purposes.

Some strategies, which, however, are not conclusive, will be discussed below.

USE OF EXISTING BUILDINGS

A very important approach for fundamentally reducing the consumption of resources is to make use of existing buildings. Compared to a building conversion, constructing a new building consumes multiple resources, even just for the shell construction, and generates many more tons of CO_2, which can only be compensated after many decades, if at all > Fig. 22.

Existing building fabric can be used as a resource in two different ways. Initially, these buildings represent an existing spatial resource, often having undergone a long payback phase. Ideally, this resource should persist in its current use or be transformed to serve a new purpose for as long as possible. In cases where a building can no longer be used or transformed, the next step is to use it as a source of building materials.
> Chapter Recyclability and Reuse

Continued use

As long as a building remains unchanged in its use, it only consumes resources such as energy, heat, and other utilities, which can, however, be minimized through climate-neutral production methods. A new investment in resources only takes place once changes are made to the building. Sustaining the use of a building through intelligent design is, therefore, one of the most climate-smart ways of creating re-configured space.

In this process, the focus should be on transforming a building to accommodate a new purpose while maintaining flexibility for future modifications.

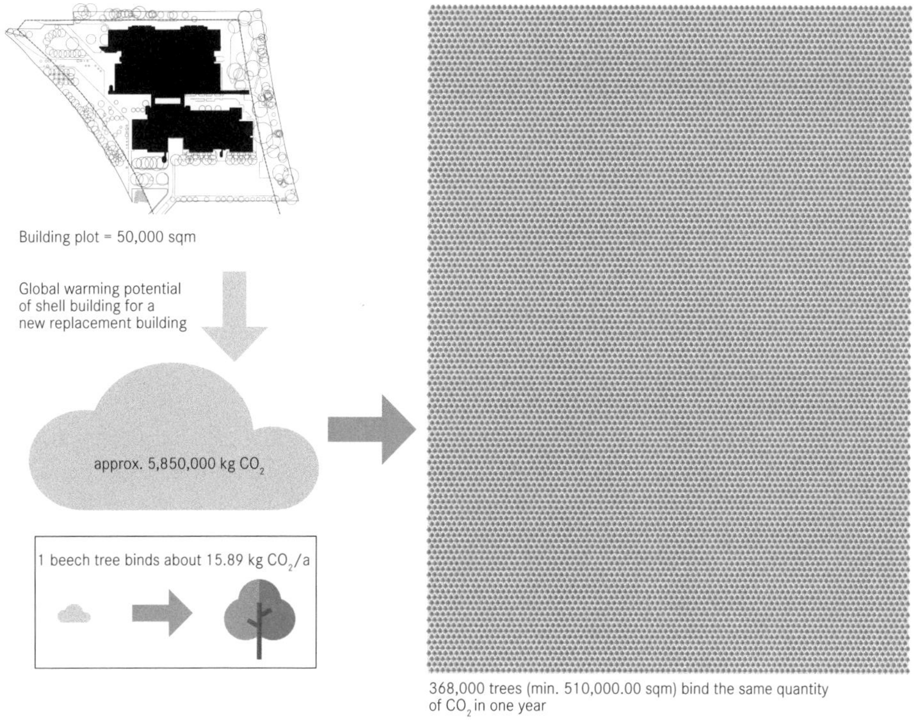

Fig. 22: CO_2 offset measures employed to compensate for the demolition of an existing school complex and construction of a new one

Minimally invasive modifications

Wherever possible, interventions should be limited to what is absolutely necessary. The project team should discuss showcasing the history of the existing building rather than transforming it to look like a new one.

■

● **Example**: A redesign may become necessary when the previous uses, such as industry, culture, or leisure, are no longer viable, the floor plan no longer meets current needs, and there are no potential users.

■ **Tip**: It is often the case that specified room schedules do not fit the existing structure of the building; for example, an area of 17 m^2 is specified for an office, but the existing building only has rooms measuring 20 m^2. In this case, it is worth reconsidering the brief in light of the existing building rather than having to carry out extensive interventions.

The objective is to use as much of the existing building fabric as possible on a permanent basis. If that is not possible, recycling should be considered to continue using building materials and components. For example, components such as doors that are no longer needed may be usefully reused in a different project; swapping resources between different projects can be a way of diversifying the design.

VALUE OF EXISTING BUILDINGS

The discussion about the continued use of existing buildings raises a new understanding of value. The value of historic/protected buildings is already a common good of society; understanding the value inherent in existing structures needs to be extended to everyday architecture. ○

As a rule, architects can make suggestions regarding a certain design style. However, the owner of the building needs to decide whether – and to what extent – the use of a building should be continued. This means that a public discussion about our building culture is necessary in order to see existing everyday architecture from a new point of view and recognize it sufficiently as a starting point for a project. ■

Everyday architecture

The architecture of the previous century is often marked by its optimization for function and construction tailored to specific uses. The structural loads, spans, story heights, staircase widths, window arrangements, etc., may, therefore, present limits or at least obstacles regarding the reuse of the building. Nevertheless, this also provides the opportunity to use existing structures for a new use scenario with clearly better space quality than a new building would offer and to combine new elements with existing structures. Since the building design has yet to be optimized for the new use, the resulting spaces often feature a rich character and identity. To achieve this, the existing structure must be transformed with care and respect. Working as an architect on an existing building should not give rise to worries and concerns over the conversion task. Instead, it should encourage an effort to understand and recognize the history of an existing building in the context of its lifecycle.

○ **Note**: The proportion of buildings protected as historic monuments in Germany is only 2.9% of all existing structures. In these cases, the approach to protecting the buildings includes repair, retention of building substance for as long as possible, careful adaptation in the case of changes of use, and retention of the building's character. The expertise is available to apply these approaches to everyday architecture as well.

■ **Tip**: During their lifecycles, buildings often change due to refurbishment or repairs to such an extent that the original design can no longer be clearly discerned. It can, therefore, be helpful to resort to old photographs or drawings from the construction period to detect and convey the original qualities.

If a building has reached the age of 60 to 80 years, it has proven its worth in terms of its structure, layout design, and construction. Anything done to this building as part of a transformation should be comparable to its existing inherent quality and should be aimed at a similar service life and resilience.

Legitimization through age

Even when the architectural quality of a building is not at first recognizable, every building is a witness of its time and features details and design principles that are typical for its period. Likewise, it is possible that a building is a component in an urban context or, together with other buildings from the same period, forms an ensemble typical of its time without itself standing out in any particular way. Last but not least, there is a certain inherent quality in an existing building simply because the building substance of the shell structure offers a good basis for climate-smart transformation.

In many existing construction methods, aspects such as longevity, reversibility, changeability, dismantlability, repairability, and resilience to environmental and use impacts are taken into account. These aspects were designed to be resilient and robust to a certain degree. Sometimes, this is because, at the time of construction, the availability of resources was limited and yet to be technically optimized to the degree that is the case in contemporary construction methods. Furthermore, many contemporary construction methods have been perfected to the degree that, while effectively serving their intended purpose, even minor inaccuracies in the building execution can result in building defects. These methods offer limited flexibility to cope with various environmental or use conditions. Therefore, developing sustainable, durable, and resilient construction methods involves examining the construction principles of existing buildings or components and assessing these for applicability to current standards.

Resilient construction methods

Therefore, it is imperative to approach an existing building with empathy and respect, analyze its design and construction principles, and transform the existing structures in a sensitive and differentiated way. To a certain degree, this also involves a paradigm shift for architects, who need to consider themselves protectors of existing buildings rather than pure designers when they wish to have the necessary expertise to work on existing buildings. When working on an existing building, this defines the scope and the basis of the future design, and a creative dialogue is needed regarding the context and the building. It may be appropriate to consider various design tools, such as overlaying, continuation, contrasting, or adaptation.

Approach to work on existing buildings

CIRCULAR CONSTRUCTION

In addition to using existing buildings, it is generally important in the design process to focus on using resources and the associated material flows, which have to be massively reduced compared to existing approaches to design and construction. Since industrialization and the start of mass production, consumption patterns have changed drastically. Rather than using resources, materials, and products for as long as possible and reusing them elsewhere when they become redundant, a linear use pattern has been established in which the intervals between production, use, and disposal become shorter and shorter > Fig. 23. Products are no longer discarded because they no longer function or can no longer be repaired but because newer and better alternatives are available. The emphasis has shifted from providing for genuine needs to generating and serving status-induced needs. This way of life, referred to as hyper-con-

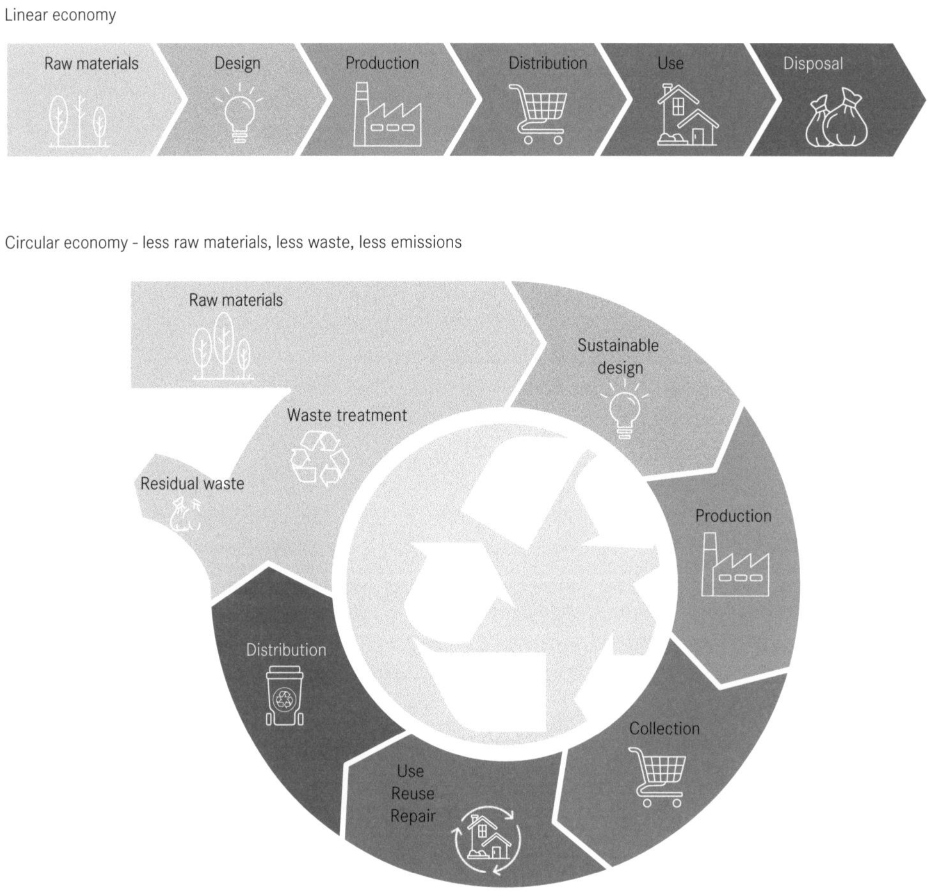

Fig. 23: Linear consumption and circular use

sumerism, is not aligned with basic social needs but focuses on the available purchasing power of people and the socially accepted idea of success.

As a society, we need to counter this phenomenon with new values to bring about a paradigm shift in resource wastage in everyday life. Buildings make an important contribution in this context because – as described above – they represent a dominant proportion of resource use. For this reason, we will discuss the principles of the circular construction industry below.

Circular economy

To avoid having to constantly rely on new resources and materials, it is imperative to think of construction in the future as a circular economy. In this context, a crucial principle should be to abandon the assumption of limitless materials and resource availability. Instead, we must prioritize exploring possibilities for sourcing and reusing existing resources > Fig. 24. Given that the production of new materials and substances used in construction contribute significantly to ongoing climate change, newly produced building materials should preferably be used only when no existing or recycled resources are available. When selecting newly manufactured building materials, it makes sense to choose materials that prioritize resource efficiency in the manufacturing processes. In addition, these materials should be used in a manner that facilitates reuse in the future.

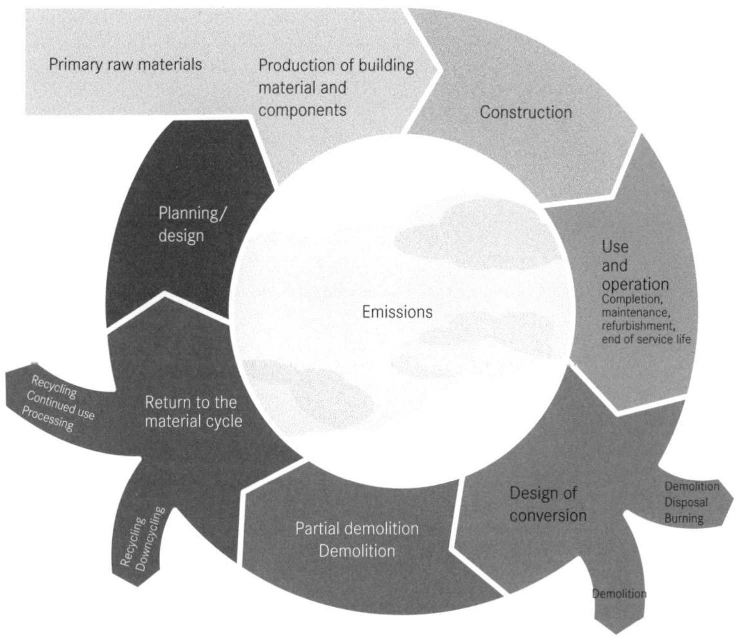

Fig. 24: Principle of a circular construction economy

RECYCLABILITY AND REUSE

For some decades efforts have been made, using various approaches, to achieve consistent recyclability of building materials and constructions. ●

Unfortunately, most construction projects are based on exactly the opposite principle. For energy efficiency, buildings have been constructed using adhesives, sealants, foils, and increasingly complex layered compounds to achieve maximum airtightness, which necessitated further technical solutions, such as controlled ventilation. With more recent buildings in particular, it tends to be challenging to correctly sort materials during demolition, which means that recycling these materials is difficult and expensive. ■

Downcycling/ upcycling

Since many of the building components used in existing structures were not initially designed for recyclability, it is difficult to achieve a circular economy. This is because many of these components cannot be reused in the same manner as before, often leading to a situation where materials are simply discarded as waste rather than used as a resource. Instead, the aim should be to reuse materials in a function of equal or increased value, a process known as upcycling. Where it is not possible to reuse a material in an equivalent function, it may be possible to use it in a less valuable form, referred to as downcycling. ●

Obstacles to recycling

It is usually not that easy to use recycling material (RC). Instead, a dedicated effort is often required, and complications may also be encountered. Where upcycled materials such as doors or windows are planned, one cannot always be certain that these components will be available at the time of construction. Therefore, it is important to keep one's design processes appropriately flexible. ■

In addition, the official regulations in many countries stipulate that only new or certified material may be used in construction, which means that recycling material must be tested and certified before it can be used. In many cases, building components in their original condition no longer comply with current regulations or building physics specifications, so a creative approach is needed when reusing them. Another issue is liability;

● **Example**: Various certificates, such as Cradle to Cradle, are based on using only materials that can be reintegrated into the cycle at the end of the use phase. However, owing to the progressively changing climate, we are now in a situation in which we must intervene in the cycle earlier and limit the amount of new building materials we use.

■ **Tip**: With new buildings, it is important to use construction techniques that do not require the permanent bonding of building materials. This is the only way to ensure that, in the future, these materials can be reused individually or that any defective materials can be removed and sorted correctly.

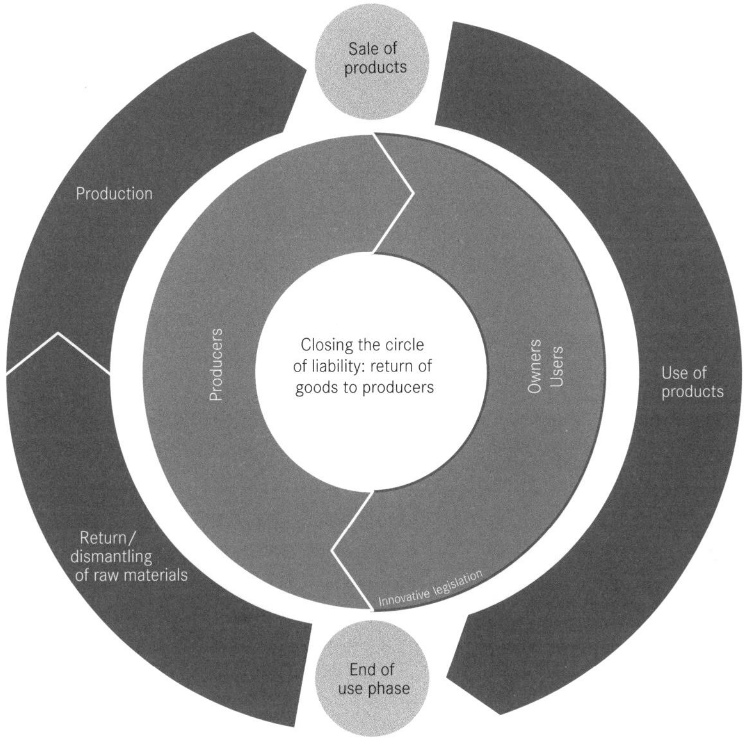

Fig. 25: Standardized circular economy in construction

it is not always clear who is responsible for guaranteeing the suitability for purpose and functional capability of used building materials. Certification makes it easier to determine where building products are reprocessed by the building material industry. > Fig. 25

● **Example**: Broken-down mineral material from brick walls or concrete components is often used as recycling material (RC), for example, in the substructure of buildings or roads. Alternatively, this material can be used as aggregate in new reinforced concrete components. This is a typical example of downcycling.

■ **Tip**: At the local level, one can find various building component and recycling centers, and there are many online suppliers and platforms available (such as www.rotordc.com, www.concular.com, www.restado.de, www.madaster.com). The market for used building materials is still relatively small but will grow considerably in the future and spawn new forms of trading.

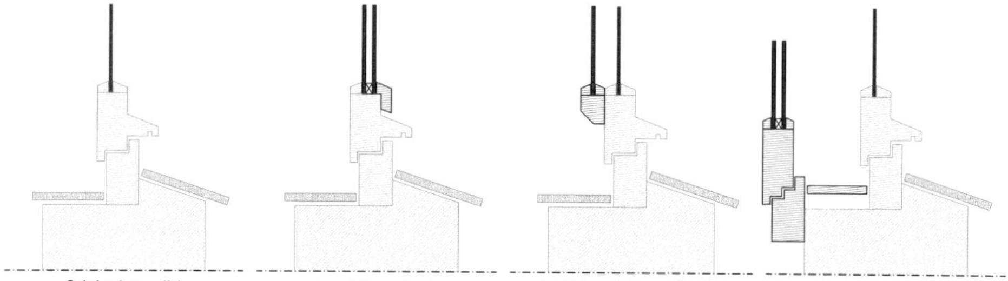

Fig. 26: Upcycling old window frames

Many building components need to be dealt with creatively. For example, old windows no longer comply with current energy conservation and airtightness standards. However, if they are installed as a secondary element in a box-type window, it may be possible to meet current regulations even with old windows > Fig. 26.

A fundamental principle in using building materials should be that discarded material is not considered waste unless it is no longer usable.

URBAN MINING

If we look beyond the resources involved in the design of a single building and extend our focus to include entire cities and regions, there is a huge amount of potentially available building material, which can and should be used as the basis of a circular economy in construction. This course of action, referred to as urban mining, aims to use existing resources and establish a second-hand culture in the construction industry. ○

SIMPLE CONSTRUCTION

Vernacular architecture

The analysis of the construction methods used in historical buildings of certain regions (also referred to as vernacular architecture) reveals that, as a rule, they were effective at coping with the respective climate

○ **Note:** Existing waste tips, formerly used as depositories for waste material and considered unavoidable hazards, are increasingly considered storage places of [usable] resources. It remains to be seen whether it will be possible to mine existing waste tips and process the materials as a viable alternative to the extraction of raw materials.

of the area using simple construction details and clear jointing principles. This is not to say that these construction methods meet current functional requirements or that they can simply be re-adopted without further consideration. However, in many cases, adopting the basic principles of vernacular architecture is possible. Using an external wall as an example > Fig. 27, we see that such a structurally optimized wall with an external thermal insulating composite system (ETICS) may consist of ten different layers or construction elements, all optimized for a specific location and mostly bonded together. However, the same thermal insulation properties can be achieved in a single layer of mineral-based, porous insulation material or with timber components and layers of clay. These alternatives offer considerable advantages in terms of building physics properties, recyclability, resilience to installation inaccuracies, and the ability to separate them into distinct source materials during demolition.

Simple construction

One may, therefore, choose to focus on simple construction as a strategy. The objective here is to comply with current requirements for thermal insulation, comfort levels, etc., using simple building materials and simple construction details. There is no doubt that, in principle, this is feasible; however, simple construction solutions are not always the most cost-effective. In many cases, the technical optimization of building materials leads to shortened installation periods, reduced drying

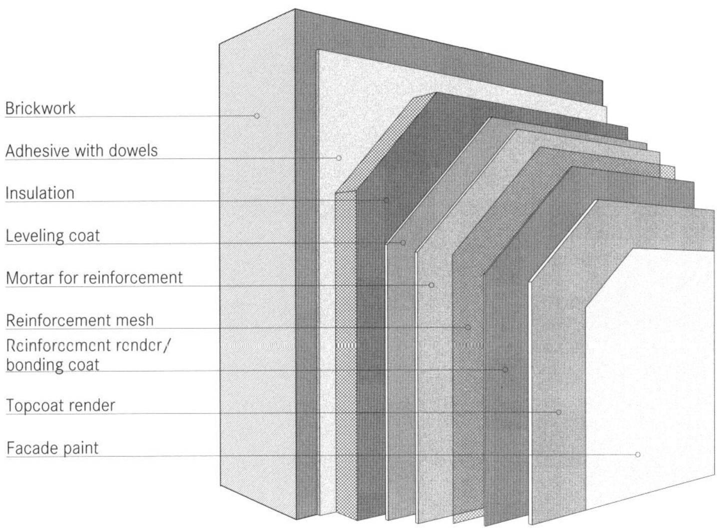

Fig. 27: Layers of an external wall

Fig. 28: Examples of vernacular construction methods

times, and the ability to install during poor weather conditions, all contributing to more economical constructions. Furthermore, traditional building materials cannot always be obtained as mass products in the market, which means that they are not competitively priced because they are more expensive to produce. But the more such building materials are in demand in the future, the more the costs will come down due to the professionalization of the manufacturing processes. ●

REDUCTION

Another strategy can be to achieve the desired aim while minimizing the consumption of resources. This can be done using three different approaches: sufficiency, consistency, and efficiency > Fig. 29.

Sufficiency

Under the heading "sufficiency" we ask how many resources are necessary to fulfill a particular (basic) need. The focus is primarily on sustainable consumption patterns and the appropriateness of consumption, particularly that of the affluent part of the global population. How much

● **Example**: Constructing a rammed earth wall using local clay, which might even be available for free at or near the building site, is one of the most sustainable methods of building a wall. However, because the clay has to be dug out and prepared, and then manually laid in layers - with interruptions to allow for drying phases - the work is very time-consuming and labor-intensive, making the wall a costly building component. On the upside, some suppliers offer prefabricated rammed earth walls, significantly reducing the labor input required on site.

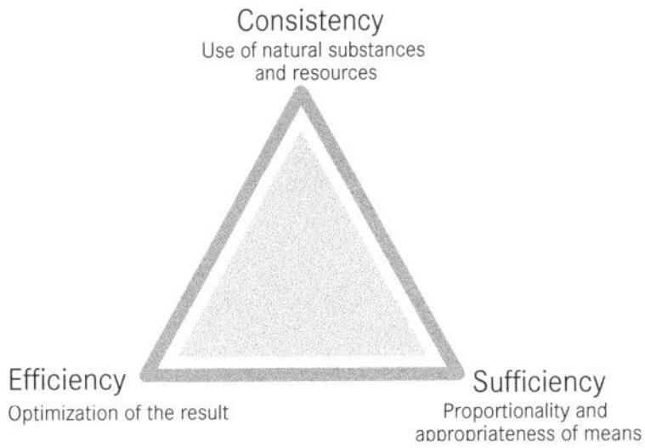

Fig. 29: The magic triangle: sufficiency, consistency, and efficiency

do we need to consume to maintain our living standards? This question can also be asked in the context of building development and should, therefore, be tabled early on during the project development phase. By questioning standardized room schedules, it is often possible to optimize the space provided; by questioning whether it is really necessary to replace an existing building with a new one, it may be possible to retain and adapt the existing structure and preserve a large amount of resource materials. ○

This principle continues during the design phase; materials and their qualities must be examined to ensure they achieve the desired aim. In some ways, sufficiency strategies work against the principles of a market economy and status-oriented thinking in our society, which is why it is often necessary for the respective architects, clients, and users to work together and clarify the appropriateness of the proposed measures. ■

Using sufficiency strategies is a crucial approach on the path to climate-smart construction.

○ **Note**: When planning a new building, significantly more resources can be saved by reducing the allocated space than by implementing a design that maximizes energy efficiency (for example). This is because a portion of the potential building mass remains unused initially, resulting in reduced operational consumption later on. Therefore, in every project, a high priority should be given to the question: "What is really necessary and makes sense?"

■ **Tip**: Projects often spring from an urgent need, so space requirements are pitched to the highest level possible. In this case, users may acquire a better and more realistic understanding of their needs if given the chance to experience and compare physical spaces that are appropriately sized for the intended purpose. Furthermore, it is preferable to avoid rooms that are only used for a single purpose during short phases; this can be done by considering multifunctional uses and by analyzing the sequence of processes in greater detail.

Consistency

Another component on the path to sustainability is consistency. In essence, consistency aims to replicate nature's material flow processes without destroying or exploiting them. When applied to building construction, the use of locally available clay is an example of a consistent construction method because, at the end of its service life, the clay can be reintroduced to the natural cycle.

However, this strategy can also be understood and applied in a wider sense. Using primarily natural building products that are locally available contributes to a circular approach. Furthermore, there are no long ● transport routes, which would incur unnecessary consumption.

It is also possible to apply the consistency strategy to construction methods adapted to local building traditions from more sustainable building eras to cope with the region's climate and allow materials to be returned to the material flow cycles via reversible additions.

Efficiency

In essence, efficiency aims to optimize the use of resources and energy. The underlying idea is not to waste resources but to get the maximum possible benefit from them.

Since efficiency is the only strategy that does not conflict with the growth strategies of our market economy, efficiency has been the fundamental principle of construction- and energy-related legislation in many countries. Of the three strategies - sufficiency, consistency, and efficiency - it is the weakest as it does not try to reduce the consumption of resources but instead aims to use them as efficiently as possible. Therefore, although important, efficiency should be applied in conjunction with the other two strategies.

The tipping points encountered when trying to increase efficiency pose another problem associated with the efficiency strategy; these are points at which the reduction in the amount of resources consumed leads to greater follow-on costs that outweigh the actual saving in terms of

● **Example**: A locally extracted natural stone has the advantage of being CO_2 neutral, except for the extraction process and the short transport route. By contrast, natural stone imported from another continent necessitates extended supply chains. There may be a lack of processing facilities at the source site, or working conditions may be problematic, requiring ships to take the material to a port from where it can be transported to the final processing location. This is then followed by longer transport routes, possibly to other countries, where the final transport takes place via HGV (Heavy Goods Vehicle).

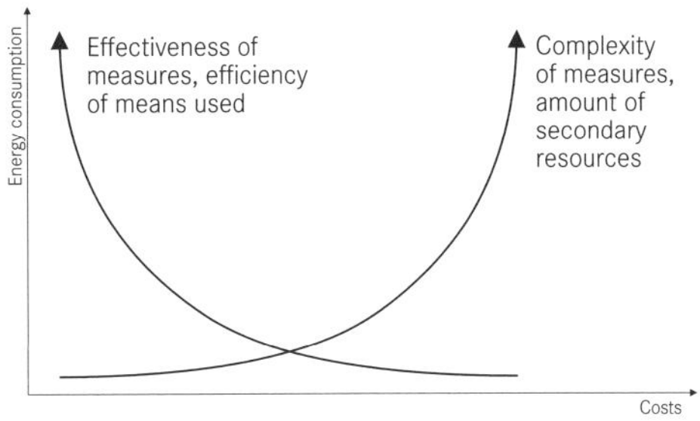

Fig. 30: Tipping point of efficiency measures

resources or energy over the lifecycle > Fig. 30. For example, a thin layer of insulation (8 cm thick) applied to an external wall that was not insulated before will improve energy efficiency in terms of heat loss. But suppose that an 8 cm thick layer of insulation is added to a wall with 18 cm of insulation, resulting in an overall thickness of 26 cm. In that case, the calculated improvement in energy efficiency is only marginal and may be further reduced by leakages, ventilation heat losses, etc. ○

In addition, there is a phenomenon known as the rebound effect, which occurs when the expected gains in efficiency are reduced due to higher expectations of comfort or changes in user behavior. ●

○ **Note:** This phenomenon is often referred to as the Pareto principle or the 80/20 rule. The theory is named after Vilfredo Pareto and states that 80 percent of consequences come from 20 percent of causes. To achieve the last 20 percent, 80 percent of effort is required. For this reason, the principle of sufficiency should also be taken into account when pursuing a strategy of efficiency.

● **Example:** If a building can only be heated in winter at great expense due to a lack of insulation, the users will tend to use only a few rooms and heat them as required. If a building is well insulated and equipped with automated technical installations, the users will typically heat all rooms to a constant temperature of 22 to 24 °C, which means that part of the energy saved through insulation is consumed to provide the users with greater comfort.

CONSTRUCTION METHOD

The construction method of a building is an important aspect in the design of sustainable and climate-smart buildings. The construction method needs to comply with various requirements, as described below.

There is the fundamental fact that different parts of a building have different life expectancies. Whereas the actual loadbearing structure has the longest service life, and all other components take the service life of the loadbearing structure as their guide, other parts of a building, such as facades, screed, or plaster, have a lifecycle that, although long-lasting, are not infinite. Surface finishes such as flooring or paint coating must be replaced significantly more frequently due to wear and tear. In contrast, the service life of technical installations can vary greatly depending on the availability of spare parts and due to changes in personal or legal requirements > Fig. 31. Consequently, the different layers in building construction should be fitted with a view to their respective lifecycle, and technical installations should be easily accessible.

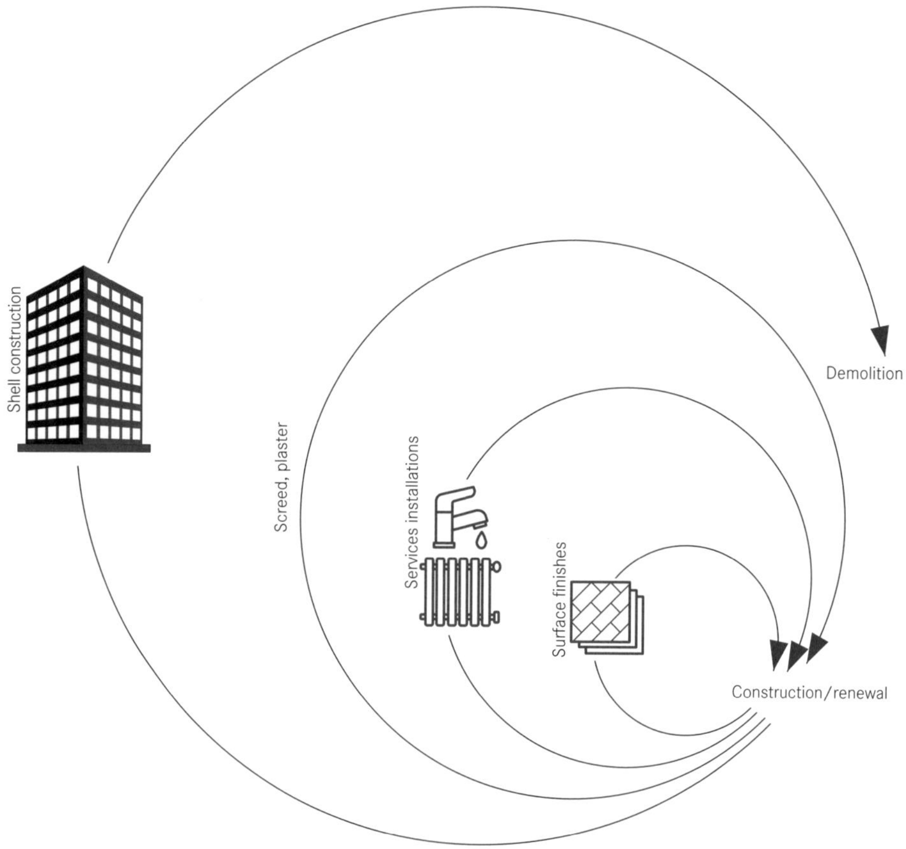

Fig. 31: Lifecycle of building components

Durability

The longer a material is in place, the better the return on the investment in terms of money and energy and resource consumption. That is why it always pays to work with durable materials and construction details when it comes to climate-appropriate construction > Fig. 32.

However, the lifecycle of the materials used in different layers varies greatly. On the one hand, there is the fact that - owing to their chemical composition - materials will age independently of external influences. For example, sealing compound will become brittle and no longer perform its function. Furthermore, external influences have an aging effect on material or might even destroy it. For example, the impact of weather or salt over the years could increase the carbonization of reinforced concrete, leading to corrosion of the reinforcement and eventually causing the component to lose its structural properties. Similarly, floor finishes and paint coatings will suffer from wear and tear, making them obsolete at some stage. ●

It is preferable to select materials without any inherent bias because materials are often deemed to possess certain properties without any factual proof.

Fig. 32: Comparison of the lifecycle of different facade materials

Building component/material	Service life in years	Frequency of replacement over 50 years
Brick, calcium silicate stone	>50	0
Fair-faced concrete	>50	0
Natural stone, manufactured stone	>50	0
Hard cladding materials bonded to thermal insulation	30	1
External thermal insulation composite system	20-40	1-2
Timber cladding: softwood	30-40	1
Wood shingles	>50	0
Metal cladding (zinc, aluminum, stainless steel)	>50	0

● **Example:** Timber is no less durable as a construction material than the solid materials in a concrete or brick building, provided it is adequately protected from moisture and sound construction details are used. Evidence of this can be seen in many towns, where the historic centers consist of centuries-old half-timbered houses that have endured the ravages of time.

Fig. 33: Durability of different construction materials

Building component/material	Service life in years	Frequency of replacement over 50 years
Floor slab	>50	0
Sealants against rising damp, groundwater	30–50	1
Solid walls	>50	0
Timber walls	>50	0
High-quality doors	>50	0
Standard doors	35–40	1
Wood, aluminum, steel windows	>50	0
Plastic windows	40	1
Locks/fittings	20–30	1–2
Sealants	10–20	2–4
External render	30–45	1
Internal plaster	>50	0
Paint coats	5–15	3–9
Screeds	>50	0
Natural/artificial stone flooring, tiles	>50	0
Textile finishes	10	4
Linoleum, caoutchouc, PVC	20	2
Flat roof sealing systems	20–40	1–2
Slate, tile, zinc, copper roofing materials	>50	0

Repairability

When selecting materials and construction details, the aim should be to ensure repairability to maintain functionality in the case of damage or defects. It is, of course, possible to replace materials later for a number of different reasons, but this should not be forced upon the user through the use of material or construction detailing that has a short service life. When using durable and repairable materials, there is a greater chance that they will have a long service life. ○

Example: external wall

Often, the repairability of building components cannot immediately be determined. For example, if a reinforced concrete component suffers

○ **Note**: Often, materials and components in existing buildings are replaced because of users' esthetic preferences. Therefore, materials should not be selected exclusively for their technical properties but also for their enduring esthetic appeal.

Fig. 34: Examples showing the repair of reinforced concrete and timber structures

from corrosion problems, repair work will involve removing the surface concrete, repairing and protecting the reinforcements, and applying a special mortar – which all together is very expensive. By contrast, if a timber beam in a half-timbered building is damaged, that damage can be repaired by simply replacing the adjoining elements > Fig. 34. It could be necessary to dismantle or remove the outer layers of a multi-layer building component in case the problem is caused by one of the layers. For example, when replacing a defective layer of thermal insulation in an external wall, the entire external insulation composite system must be replaced. Bonded joints can only be undone using expensive methods. A curtain wall, on the other hand, can be dismantled and – in a best-case scenario – be refitted without loss once the insulation has been replaced.

Example: floor finishes

The repairability of finishes subject to wear, such as floor finishes, also varies greatly. For example, PVC flooring usually consists of a carrier layer and an upper decorative layer, which, when damaged, cannot always be repaired. Linoleum, on the other hand, is a pure, natural, solid-colored product that can be used for decades if maintained properly. Scratches and tears can always be repaired or retouched, which means there is no need to replace and install a new flooring finish.

Example: services installations

Repairability is also an important aspect of service installations. On the one hand, it is imperative to ensure that wear parts such as valves, flaps, sensors, and controllers are accessible for repair. On the other hand, it is important to select technical installations considering how long spare parts can still be supplied and how easy it is to repair the installation.

Unfortunately, many building components currently available in the building products market were not designed for repairability but for minimal production costs. This means many building components – such as door leaves – must be replaced when damaged. Therefore, it is important to investigate the manufacturer's reasons for choosing the composition and construction of the respective building components. Taking

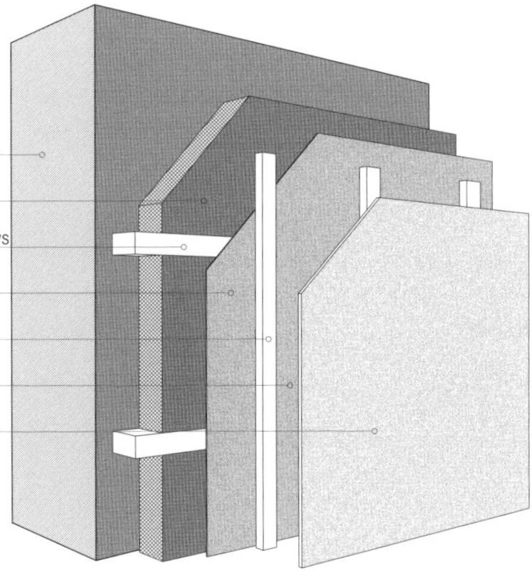

Fig. 35: Fully selectable and dismantlable curtain wall facades

this kind of action will make manufacturers understand that longevity ○ and repairability are quality criteria.

Dismantlability and selectability

In addition to repairability, it is important that materials and building components can be dismantled with the least possible damage and that individual materials can be selected. With multi-layer building components, it is particularly important to be able to separate layers without damaging material to facilitate far-reaching recyclability > Fig. 35.

Sometimes, it is not possible to avoid replacing building components or individual layers; the reasons may be changes in use, wear and tear, new regulations, or damage during the lifecycle. This means that the dismantling and reinstallation of components and materials should be considered in every design and made possible with the appropriate construction details. ■

○ **Note**: Lawmakers are increasingly discussing a right to repair. Likewise, many manufacturers are changing their approach; they offer guarantees that they will accept the return of materials for recycling; recycled materials are increasingly integrated into production processes; assembly systems are offered that allow for damage-free dismantling, etc. Architects should actively make inquiries regarding these issues.

■ **Tip**: Dismantlable solutions are also available for building components that, at first glance, do not seem to be dismantlable. For example, connection elements are offered for installing facing brick skins that do not require mortar and can be reused repeatedly. Some screeds are also dry systems installed with tongue and groove, etc.

Lightweight construction

Another option is to significantly reduce the building mass used. Even though it is impossible to directly correlate the weight and quantity of the building materials used to a CO_2 equivalent, the sparing use of materials generally helps to reduce the consumption of resources. Using a lightweight construction can be a way of optimizing the required properties of a particular building component. For example, rather than building a continuous solid wall, the structural load transfer is managed via columns, and the intermediate space is filled with panels and layers of insulation material, which means that all sound and thermal insulation requirements are met. This helps to significantly reduce the building mass, and it is possible to make changes and selectively remove materials without major interference with the building fabric during the building's lifecycle.

At the same time, the reduced weight of the building components means that less load has to be transferred and supported by the foundations, which can also reduce the building mass of the secondary building components. ●

CHOICE OF MATERIALS

In addition to the principles of jointing and construction, the criteria for choosing materials are explained below.

Natural building materials

One of the best options for achieving consistency > Chapter Climate-Smart Strategies/Reduction is to use natural building materials. Provided they are not industrially modified or chemically changed, natural building materials such as timber, clay, and natural stone are essentially free from noxious substances, recyclable, and – with the exception of the extraction, preparation, and transport processes – CO_2 neutral. ○

It should be noted that owing to our current living standards, the scope for using natural building materials is limited nowadays, and these materials cannot be considered a solution for all situations. For example, buildings that consist exclusively of timber, clay, or natural stone can only be implemented on a small scale. However, natural building materials can usually be easily integrated into the design. Even when these

● **Example:** When internal and external walls are built in lightweight construction instead of brickwork, the supporting floors have less load to support, resulting in smaller dimensions and reduced load. This significantly reduces load transfer via the vertical building components, which have to be supported by the foundations and the subsoil. This means that it may be possible to avoid more expensive foundations.

○ **Note:** Building materials in existing buildings have often been chemically treated and, therefore, must be examined for noxious substances before reuse. It is also possible for natural building materials to give off noxious fumes. For example, even untreated wood may outgas volatile organic compounds (VOCs) into the room air.

are industrially treated in a secondary process, energy consumption is often much lower than in conventional approaches.

Materials with low CO_2 equivalent

As already described in the chapter on Climate Change/The Risk of Global Warming, reducing CO_2 emissions throughout the entire lifecycle of buildings is an important measure > Fig. 36. Data that include almost all manufacturers can be relied on to ascertain the energy input during the manufacture of various materials and building components.

Environmental product declaration (EPD)

The global warming potential of a product is usually assessed using the CO_2 equivalent. These days, most manufacturers provide CO_2 information for their products. Worldwide, this is structured uniformly by ISO 14025 and the European standard EN 15804. Furthermore, CO_2 equivalents are calculated based on the methods used in eco-balancing. > Chapter Evaluation Methods/Eco-Balancing and Material Flow Analysis

Sometimes, it is possible to form product groups with comparatively uniform CO_2 equivalents because the production steps of the products are largely comparable. However, there are also building components that, depending on the manufacturer or product, have very specific CO_2 emissions > Fig. 37. ●

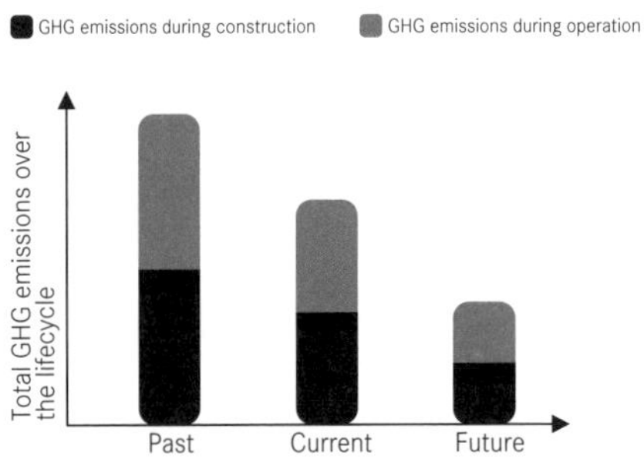

Fig. 36: Reduction of greenhouse gases

● **Example**: The CO_2 emissions of different types of face brick can vary greatly. The reason for this may be found in the firing process, the number of firings, and the type of energy used for operating the respective furnace. Similarly, multi-layer components such as curtain wall facades or drywall constructions can only be compared to a very limited extent.

Fig. 37: GWP values of selected materials for the production phase (A1-A3)

Material/building component	Kg CO_2 eq
Mineral building materials	
Calcium silicate block	126
Face brick	533
Ready-mix concrete C25/30	229
Ready-mix concrete C30/37	244
Aerated concrete	283
Rammed earth wall	9
Clay brick	94
Lightweight concrete made of expanded clay	193 to 239
Lightweight concrete made of natural pumice	46
Roof slates	15
Roof tiles	15
Fiber cement board	7
Gypsum board	1 to 3
Clay building board	0.05
Internal gypsum plaster	119
Internal lime plaster	191
Clay plaster	93
Insulation materials	
Mineral wool facade insulation	70
Mineral wool flat roof insulation	210
Mineral wool internal insulation	40
EPS (bulk density 20 kg/m³)	58
EPS (bulk density 30 kg/m³)	85
XPS	96
Woodwool slab	-29
Cellulose insulation board	-20
Cotton insulation	-1
Straw bales	-127
Timber/wood	
Solid construction timber	613 to 769
Cross laminated timber	-605 to -764
Plywood panel	-709
OSB board	-609
Thermally modified wood	-226

Material/building component	Kg CO_2 eq
Metals	
Reinforcement bar	474
Galvanized steel profiles	1363 to 2875
Steel sheeting	2453
Stainless steel sheeting	3623
Aluminum sheeting	10
Floor finishes	
PVC flooring	7
Linoleum flooring	4
Laminates	1262
Needle felt	9
Ceramic tiles and slabs	6 to 11
Coatings	
Water-based facade paint	2081
Silicone resin facade paint	1374
Water-based interior paint	3
Lime-based interior paint	1
Window gloss paint	1893
Parquet varnish	1914

Note: The above data were taken from ÖKOBAUDAT and have not been checked for accuracy or for being up to date. In some cases, the data from ÖKOBAUDAT varies significantly from the EPD data of manufacturers.

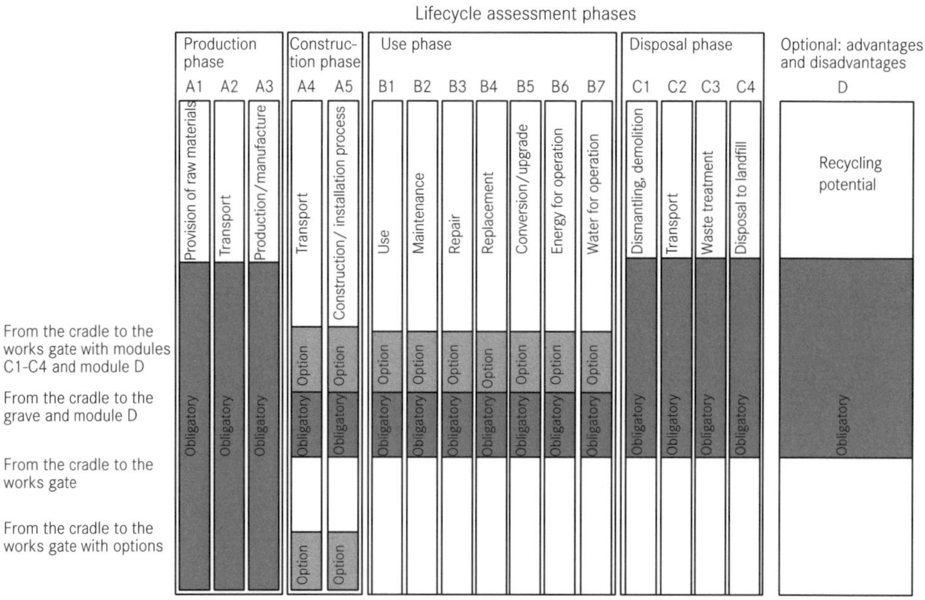

Fig. 38: EPD scope within the lifecycle in accordance with EN 15804

In an analysis, one also needs to consider the scope within the entire lifecycle of a building. The manufacturers can provide reliable data for the manufacturing phase of the building product (A1–A3) and possibly the construction phase (A4–A5). If the intention is also to consider the use phase (B1–B7) and disposal phase (C1–C4), the calculations must be based on uniform data > Fig. 38.

Scope within the lifecycle

Recyclates

Amount of waste

Waste from construction and demolition constitutes more than half of all waste. Even municipal waste or waste from trade and industry only accounts for a little more than one-fifth of the waste from construction and demolition > Fig. 39. This enormous amount reveals a huge problem associated with the linear consumption of resources in the construction industry and points to the necessity of working in a circular way using recyclates.

Downcycling in practice

For many decades, there has been an established method of recycling in which spoil from ground excavation and mineral hardcore is reused. However, this is almost exclusively carried out through downcycling > Chapter Climate-Smart Strategies/Recyclability and Reuse in groundworks and road construction, where hardcore is used as a sub-base. So, demolition material is reused but not to reduce demand for building materials in construction. Fit-out components are almost exclusively used in a linear manner > Fig. 40.

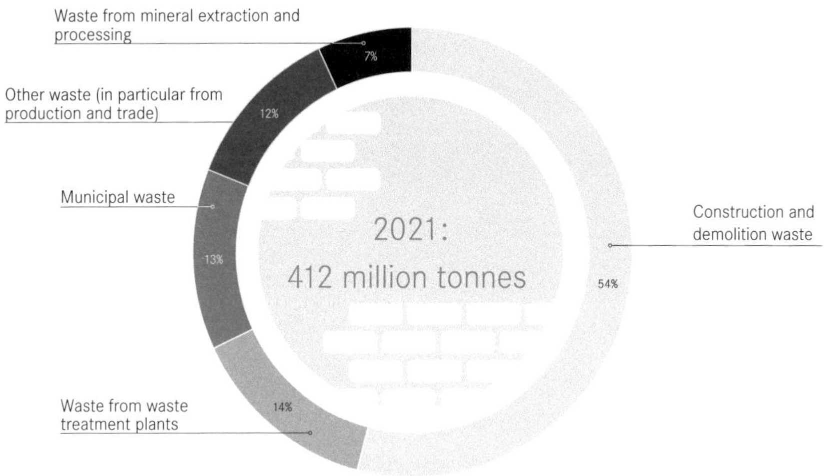

Fig. 39: Proportion of waste from various sectors in Germany

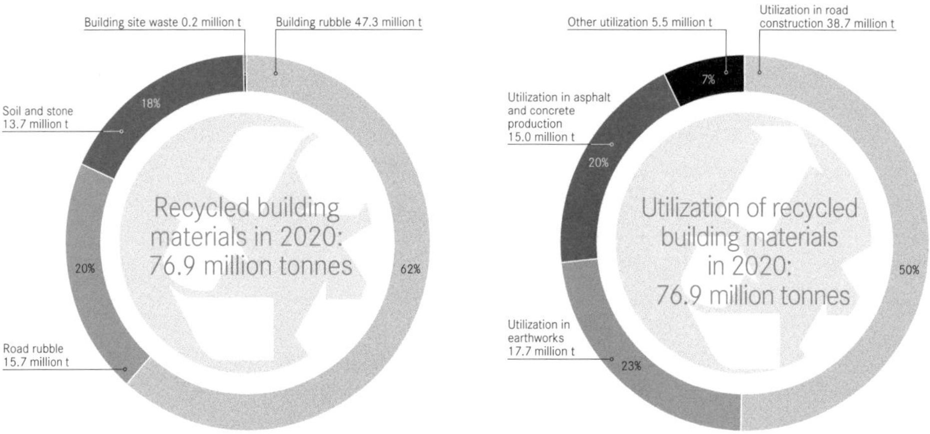

Fig. 40: Recycled building materials as a proportion of the total quantity and their uses

Upcycling in practice

To significantly reduce the consumption of resources for building materials, it is essential to reintroduce components from demolished buildings into the circular material flow. The direct reuse of building components is only possible to a very limited extent. When defects have to be made good so that the item can be reused, it is often necessary to rework or repair them. Furthermore, when building components are reworked or repaired, they must satisfy current requirements. ○

It is often difficult for architects and their clients to reuse components such as windows and doors that play a role in fire protection and are subject to approval. Firstly, the availability of such items is not assured when the building application is made. Secondly, the properties of these building components can often no longer be clearly documented, which means that the parts have to be re-tested. ●

○ **Note**: In many countries, materials and building components taken from buildings are legally declared as waste, which means they have to be re-evaluated and tested before being reused as building materials. Owing to the necessity of the transformation, these obstacles to recycling must be overcome without ignoring quality and safety aspects.

● **Example**: When drawings supporting a building application include windows, it is imperative to verify the availability of the specified window size at the time of construction (usually at least a year later). Since the market for recycled building materials is still very small, it is advisable to obtain the building materials needed from the planned demolition of a building or obtain them in advance and then store them until they are required for construction.

USE OF TECHNICAL INSTALLATIONS

Degree of mechanization in buildings

The degree of mechanization within a building and the potential installation of innovative technology are important aspects to consider. On the one hand, technical service installations help ensure that the best possible use is made of the facilities provided and that the comfort levels meet the users' requirements. On the other hand, from the point of view of the entire lifecycle, a high degree of mechanization makes a building more prone to faults. It makes the building dependent on these installations, even though - compared to the building fabric - they have a significantly shorter service life.

Objectives of services installations

Therefore, the objective of service installation design should be to try to achieve the specified comfort levels using the actual building components before resorting to service installations. ■

That being said, service installations and the automatic control of installations and systems help limit energy use to the necessary level and to avoid unproductive overcapacity. ●

High-tech versus low-tech

The choice between a high-tech and a low-tech approach must be made in every project, i.e. a decision has to be made as to what degree of mechanization is needed for the specified use. In the high-tech approach, the degree of mechanization follows the optimized specification of the functions of the facility, whereas in the low-tech approach, technical installations are only used where they are absolutely necessary. Whatever the situation, the service installations should always be designed with a view to the entire lifecycle, the service life of the individual building components, and the energy consumption of the installations over the service life.

Harnessing energy – using alternative sources of energy

Every building needs energy for electricity, heating, and possibly cooling. As already pointed out, it makes sense to reduce energy consumption by using it efficiently. > Chapter Climate-Smart Strategies/Reduction In addition, it is essential to generate the required energy in a regenerative manner. Buildings that are powered entirely with renewable energy have

■ **Tip:** If, for example, the structure is protected by building components against summer heat gain and good ventilation is ensured, there is less heat load that needs to be reduced. This means that it may be possible to omit a mechanical cooling system with its heavy and continual use of energy. Similarly, it is possible to reduce technical installations while still meeting the specified comfort levels.

● **Example:** If the lighting in secondary rooms of public buildings is controlled via manual switches, for example, in restroom facilities, lights are often on throughout the entire use period. However, if a movement sensor controls the lighting, lights will only go on when the facility is actually being used, resulting in significantly reduced energy consumption.

a minimal impact on the climate over the service life. This means that efficiency measures must also always be planned for sufficiency to achieve a sensible compromise between resource investment and usefulness over the lifecycle.

Centralized/ decentralized generation

Most municipal networks that supply buildings with electricity and possibly heat from centralized sources have grown over decades and typically distribute energy generated by the combustion of fossil fuels or nuclear power. In the future, centralized energy-generating entities will continue to play an important role, even though the energy they supply will be from renewable sources such as geothermics, wind farms, and solar power plants. In the future, supplying buildings with regenerative energy will make electricity and heat networks necessary that carry significantly higher loads. However, as existing networks are not laid out for such loads

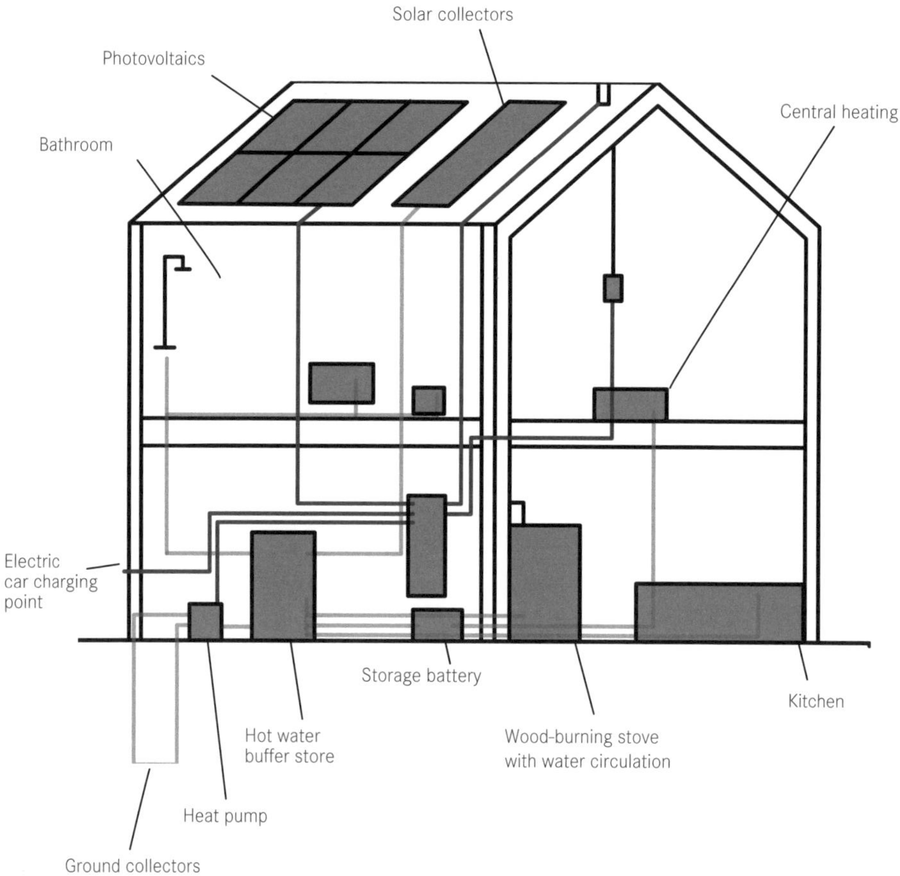

Fig. 41: Example of a building with decentralized supply

and there is only limited space available for the installation of large energy farms and plants – at least in inner city areas with their high energy consumption – it makes sense and is necessary to consider decentralized supply solutions. Any electricity and heat that is generated within a building does not have to be transported via networks with limited capacities. In addition, there is no primary energy loss during transport to the building. > Chapter Resource and Energy Consumption/Primary energy

Storing energy

When energy is generated in a decentralized facility, it may not be possible to generate the energy at the time when needed. For example, photovoltaic systems do not generate electricity at night even though electricity may be needed. In addition, there are seasonal variations; during summer, it is often possible to generate much more solar heat than required, whereas in winter, there might not be sufficient energy to heat the building adequately. This makes adequate storage capacity and/or buffer options necessary > Fig. 41.

Innovation and experimental construction

In addition to the established construction and services solutions, innovation is needed in all areas to address the challenges presented by ongoing change. This typically applies to building materials, construction methods, and services installations – but especially to new ways of thinking about building concepts and designs.

Innovative building materials

Many manufacturers of building products are working on new concepts, new products that make careful use of resources, and on improving recycling processes. In addition, there are many new developments based on natural and renewable raw materials. An example is the use of fungus mycelium for construction, which is still in the trial phase. The idea is to use fungus mycelium to form building structures that, in combination with other materials, provide great strength and are fully compostable, as well as allowing freeform design.

Fig. 42: Examples of renewable building materials

Fig. 43: Examples of innovative construction methods

Furthermore, current research focuses on fast-growing plants such as bamboo, paulownia, miscanthus, and algae to be able to provide large quantities of building materials after short cultivation periods > Fig. 42.

Innovative construction methods

Many new and innovative construction methods are also under development. Examples are growing structural systems that consist of living plants like espalier trees or replacing bonded building components with dry-jointed components such as brickwork without mortar, pallet houses, or straw bale buildings. Digital design instruments, such as parametric design, also develop exceptionally lightweight and dismantlable construction.

Lastly, it is important to renew efforts to apply experimental approaches to building construction to find new solutions to climate change challenges.

Approaches to the design process

The effort to achieve climate-smart design is intrinsic in all design phases and design areas of a building. This process, which can last several years, determines the entire lifecycle as well as the parameters of how a building can be used and the effect of future changes, through to the demolition. For this reason, architects must not only focus on the current design and construction phase and the immediate result following completion but also consider relevant issues pertinent to the entire lifecycle.

This means that it is important to reach an agreement with all specialist engineers and the building owner regarding climate protection goals and continually discuss new improvements. Below, we will address various approaches and control mechanisms employed within the design process.

TOWN PLANNING APPROACHES

At the level of town planning, several issues need to be considered in conjunction. For example, at the scale of individual buildings, existing situations should be used for as long as possible because every change involves the emission of greenhouse gases and the consumption of resources. However, the retention of urban quarters and social structures may also require intervention; for example, when changing needs must be met, adverse developments averted, or structures modified because they simply are no longer appropriate. There is also the fact that many of the world's regions are under enormous pressure to provide housing and infrastructure due to growing populations and demographic changes.

Climate consequences in the city

Climate change has given rise to phenomena that require a new orientation in town planning. Some towns and cities can no longer cope with rapidly changing - and sometimes extreme - weather events, such as heat waves, heavy rain, flooding, or storms, which means that, to cope with these events, they must be made resilient.

For example, it is possible to counteract the effect of heat events by planting on and around buildings and urban spaces, installing shading devices, providing places of respite for people, and creating fresh air avenues that allow cooler air into the city. ■

■ **Tip**: Cities are usually significantly hotter than rural areas. To retain the residential and functional attractiveness of cities, it is very important to ensure that a contribution is made to the urban climate, not just in the context of town planning but with each project. This can be achieved by greening roofs and facades, reducing heat-storing items in the open, ensuring that soil sealing is avoided where possible, and reducing heat emission, for example, from air-conditioning systems.

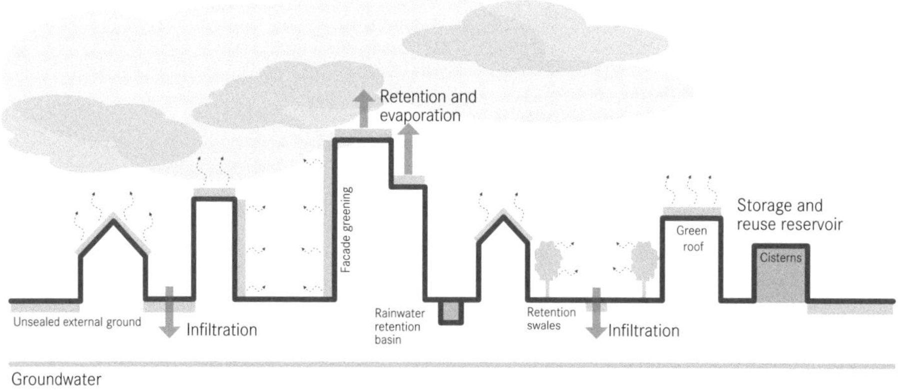

Fig. 44: Options for retaining flood water in sponge cities

In addition to effective sewer systems with the capacity to drain large quantities of water, heavy rain events can be dealt with by removing surfaces that seal the soil so that rainwater can drain into the ground where it occurs and by establishing retention facilities for the temporary retention and gradual release of water. Such facilities can take the form of specially constructed flood control basins, infiltration blocks inserted in the ground, swales for the deliberate retention of flood water, or extensive planting. O

Mobility concepts

Beyond the considerations relating to the urban climate, it is important to look at mobility concepts and plan the introduction of new forms of mobility in cities. Transport systems heavily dependent on private cars need large areas of land for traffic and parking, leading to the sealing of soil; these systems also cause heavy pollution and push out other forms of mobility and leisure activities from the public space. Hence, it is important to create high-quality leisure and green spaces as well as

O **Note**: During heavy rain events, it is imperative that the amount of water does not exceed the capacity of the sewer system and that it is fed into the system with a delay. By creating green roofs and ensuring there are open areas where the soil is not sealed, it is possible to reduce the amount of rainwater run-off considerably. The term "sponge city" has been coined in the context of planning the resilience of urban areas to heavy rain events.

Fig. 45: Transformation of urban spaces in Barcelona

Fig. 46: Examples of ad hoc measures in cities

convenient and climate-friendly mobility spaces for pedestrians, cyclists, and local public transport systems. Another critical issue in town planning is the organization of delivery logistics. Existing urban situations must accommodate the needs of all types of transport while also providing high-quality public urban areas beyond the space taken up by private cars.

Participation

When aiming to bring about change in a city, all stakeholders must engage in open dialog and possibly try out proposed measures for short periods for the purpose of evaluation because, often, the complexity of the different needs can only be grasped in a process that allows open discourse. At the same time, the background and objective of the intended urban transformation must be communicated in an open process, with sufficient flexibility regarding perceived problems, to achieve a high degree of acceptance. Sometimes, it makes sense to implement measures for a short period and then examine the effects on the urban fabric and society > Fig. 46.

PROJECT DEVELOPMENT AND SPACE REQUIREMENT PLANNING

Project development

Before work on the design begins, all essential parameters are clarified in the project development phase. At this stage, a building plot or existing building must be found, the list of requirements compiled, and funding secured. As the key project aims are defined at this stage, it is possible to clarify many parameters relating to the climate-appropriateness of the building; these will influence design and climate-related decisions in the right way from the beginning. Decisions may be made about CO_2 emissions, the consumption of resources, operating conditions (e.g. climate-neutral operation), and targets to be met for certification.

Space requirement planning

An essential process in the quest to minimize the consumption of resources is to critically review and specify space requirements. It is common practice to adopt space requirements based on previously completed projects, reference projects, and statistics data without adjusting them to the space actually needed in the respective project. An accurate analysis of the space required in a particular project, considering the principle of sufficiency, may well find that less space is required. This, in turn, will significantly reduce greenhouse gas emissions and resource investment because the provision of built space is always associated with them.

Examples of questions to be asked:

- How much space is really needed?
- Is there a difference between how much space is needed and how much space could be provided when making maximum use of the budget?
- What functions are to take place in a room?
- Will the room be used continuously or only temporarily?
- Is it possible to reduce the space requirement with the help of multifunctional utilization?
- How should rooms be designed when the reduction in space is not to be perceived as a limitation but as added value for its users?
- Is the design of spaces and rooms flexible enough to allow other uses?

When one succeeds in reducing adjoining spaces used only temporarily, good sufficiency with respect to the rooms is usually possible > Figs. 47–48.

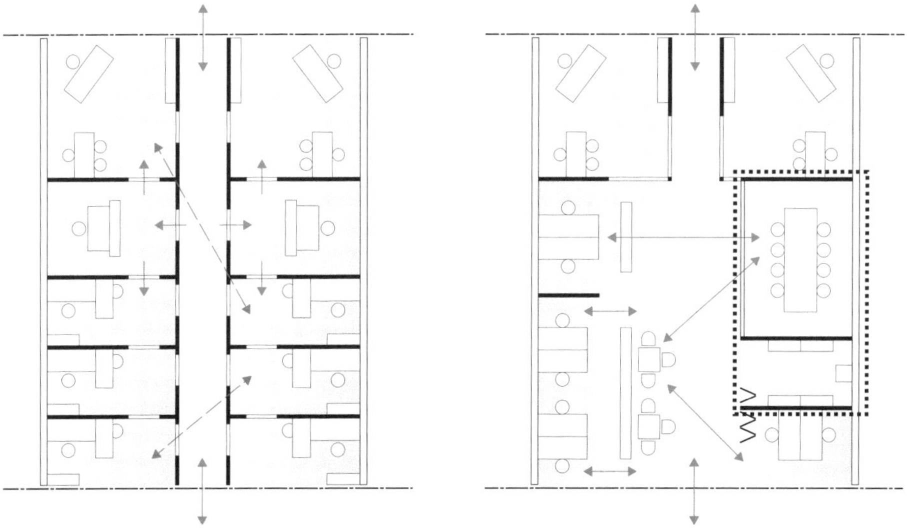

Fig. 47: Change of a cellular office layout to create multifunctional office areas

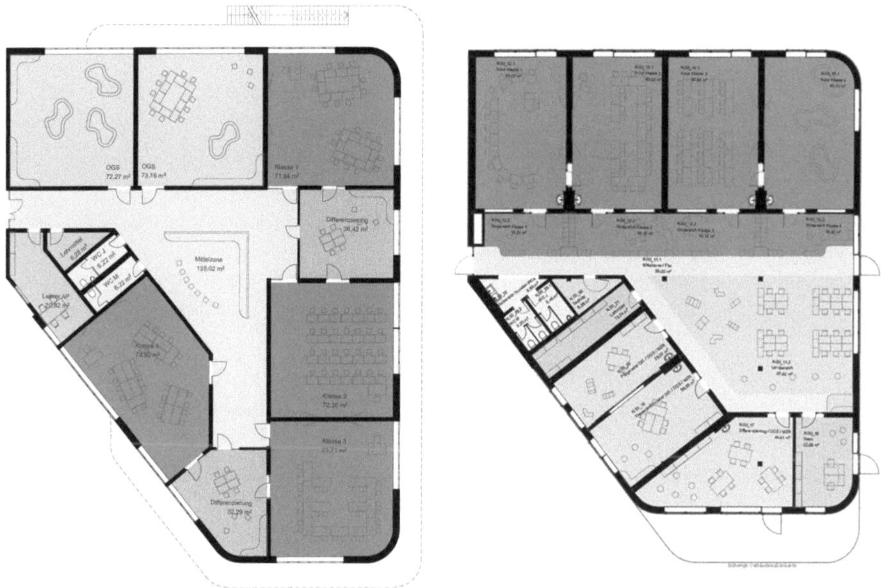

Fig. 48: Optimized layout of a school floor plan using shared learning areas

There are no universally applicable solutions for different functions, which means that the options and possibilities must be worked out again in each project. When a design is produced under the sufficiency principle, it is important to check that future users' needs and ideas are met to ensure their acceptance.

ANALYSIS OF EXISTING BUILDINGS

When an architectural project involves an existing building, it is important to conduct an in-depth analysis of the existing building fabric to ensure accuracy in the design process. The following areas should be analyzed:

- Context of a building
- Building structure
- Previous uses and/or changes
- Building/ground contamination
- Technical aspects of the building fabric

Context analysis

This analysis focuses on framework conditions such as the urban context, the applicable planning law, the type of building zoning in the neighborhood, sociocultural influences/image of the location, transport connections, and the availability of utilities. It goes without saying that this analysis is also needed for new buildings. However, owing to the evolved and changing structures of existing buildings, the framework conditions tend to be more complex and heterogeneous, which means that significantly more parameters must be considered in the design process; it may also be necessary to clear up any contradictions.

Building structure

When dealing with an existing building, it is important to understand the structural principles involved. It is often possible to obtain information about the building structure and construction details from old construction files or documents held by the original designers. If the structural calculations for the building are still available, valuable information can be gained regarding load computation, load transfer, bracing, reinforcements, steel/timber structures, and concealed components such as foundations.

Example: Creating an open "learning house" atmosphere in a school while minimizing typical classroom structures and separate after-school childcare facilities makes sense only if the teachers can and want to follow a corresponding teaching concept. Where functions work well in the rooms designed for them, unused space can sometimes be reduced while providing significantly improved individual learning settings for the children.

Example: It is possible that the zoning map for a disused industrial area still restricts the zoning to its original industrial use. This means that zoning issues have to be discussed with the municipal administration before these areas can be re-zoned and transformed for mixed use.

Previous uses and changes

The current state of the building may not always be as shown in the original documents from the time the building application was made. Usually, buildings are modified several times over the course of their lifecycle. This may involve repairs and the replacement of individual components through to a complete overhaul. If these modifications did not require a building permission, they might not be documented and must be confirmed through suitable surveys. ■

The construction file of a building will often contain information about the function of the building at the time of construction. However, this may have changed several times over the course of the building's lifecycle. One should always try to obtain information about former uses as accurately as possible because not only can this offer an indication of physical changes carried out since the time of construction, but it may also provide pointers to potential risks associated with the previous uses such as additional contamination.

Contamination analysis

When assessing whether it is possible to continue using the existing fabric of a building it is first imperative to ascertain whether any of the building's components contain contamination that must be removed from the building. Most countries have clear regulations and defined limits that must be observed. The contamination analysis will reveal how much of the building fabric will be available for the new design once the contaminated material has been removed > Figs. 49–50.

Fig. 49: Examples of noxious substances

Asbestos	(for example in ventilation ducts, ceilings, plaster, and fire protection cladding)
PCB	(polychlorinated biphenyls, for example in old lamps, joint fillers, and paints)
SMF	(synthetic mineral fibers, for example as insulation material, also for pipes)
PAH	(polycyclic aromatic hydrocarbons, for example in sealing membranes and sealants)
PHs	(petroleum hydrocarbons, for example in industrial flooring materials)
DDT	(Dichlorodiphenyltrichloroethane, for example in wall paints and wood coatings)
PCP	(Pentachlorophenol, for example as wood preservative in timber structures)
HBCD	(Hexabromocyclododecane, for example in EPS insulation material)

■ **Tip**: It is often advisable to open up building components or to carry out excavations in order to check the construction details and underlying geometry. It can also be helpful to take note of elements such as door handles, wall tiles, sanitary fittings, staircase railings, and switches, as these may be typical for a certain building period or fashion in construction. This information can then be used to draw conclusions regarding when certain changes were made.

Fig. 50: Photos of typically suspect areas

Technical assessment of the building fabric

Following analysis of the building's structure and possible contamination, it is also necessary to check the usability of the existing building fabric. Examples of questions that may be relevant for this process include the following:

- What material are the building components made of?
- What are the properties of this material?
- What else will fulfill this purpose?
- What may no longer be used in its present form?
- What is damaged or shows signs of wear?
- What can be repaired and what can be reinforced?
- Is it possible to dismantle building elements and reinstall them elsewhere?

In some cases, it is possible to assess building elements without damaging them. However, in many cases it is necessary to open up building components or damage them in order to assess concealed components such as beams or structural floors or to understand the construction of layers.

Resource catalog

In order to obtain a complete overview of the existing building, it is often helpful to compile a catalog of resources for the purpose of recording the building in its entirety. In this way it is also possible to accurately record and plan the flow of materials during conversions and adaptations.

ID of building component		Image
Recording date		
Building		
Floor / room number / room name		
Building component		

Number	
Subcategory of building component (description)	
Main material	
Other materials	
Dimensions	
Method of fitting/construction/ jointing	
Condition	
Other description (if available) Designated use, manufacturer, fire protection, age, sound protection, load-bearing or non-load-bearing component, amount of pollutants, is the component exposed to the weather?, specific classes of component, color	

Fig. 51: Example of a resource catalog

Fig. 52: Examples of designs using existing resources

DESIGN PROCESS

The framework conditions established during the project development phase take concrete shape in the design and construction phases. Normally, the design and construction steps follow a typical sequence. As the design becomes more detailed during the design process, successive decisions are made that are essential to the implementation of the objectives and to the ongoing lifecycle of the building. This applies not only to the conceptual design of buildings but also to the choice of methods and materials at various stages of the design process.

Careful use of resources in design

A fundamental question for architects is the extent to which design can or should be independent of materials and resources. Bearing in mind the finality of resources, the choice of construction materials and methods should always be made with a view to reducing CO_2 emissions as much as possible, which in turn means that this choice has an essential impact on the form and scope of design.

Decisions relating to materials and construction

When the principle of circularity is applied to construction components, this imposes limits on the design parameters and on the freedom of design. The type of composition that can be achieved with these elements is determined by their availability, geometry, and appropriateness of use. It is also important to take into account the fact that, compared to conventional construction, projects aimed at reducing CO_2 emissions and carefully using resources will have different limitations, for example with respect to loadbearing structures, spans, cantilevers, or openings. For this reason, the choice of construction method and materials should be made at an early stage.

Flexibility of use

Furthermore, the resources required to meet demand should be used in such a way that a high degree of flexibility is ensured throughout the lifecycle. Spatial requirements change over the lifecycle of a building owing to changes in user, modified needs, or lifecycle phases. This must be taken into account in the design by incorporating appropriate flexibility and adaptability. The easier it is to carry out modifications in the future,

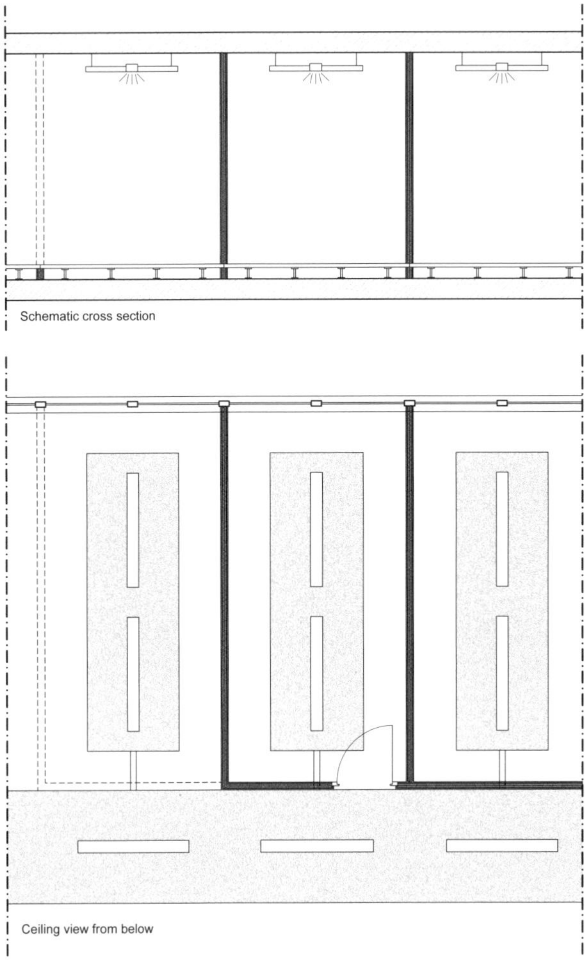

Fig. 53: Example of a flexible design of partition walls in offices

the lower will be the consumption of resources and the longer will be the service life of building components and buildings.

Observing this flexibility of use is a theme that permeates the entire design process, from the initial layout design through to the design of construction details > Fig. 53. Constructions that use layered details and dismantlable elements, and include the possibility to work on short-lived components such as wiring, piping, or control mechanisms, make it possible to carry out interventions at certain areas of the building with minimal damage.

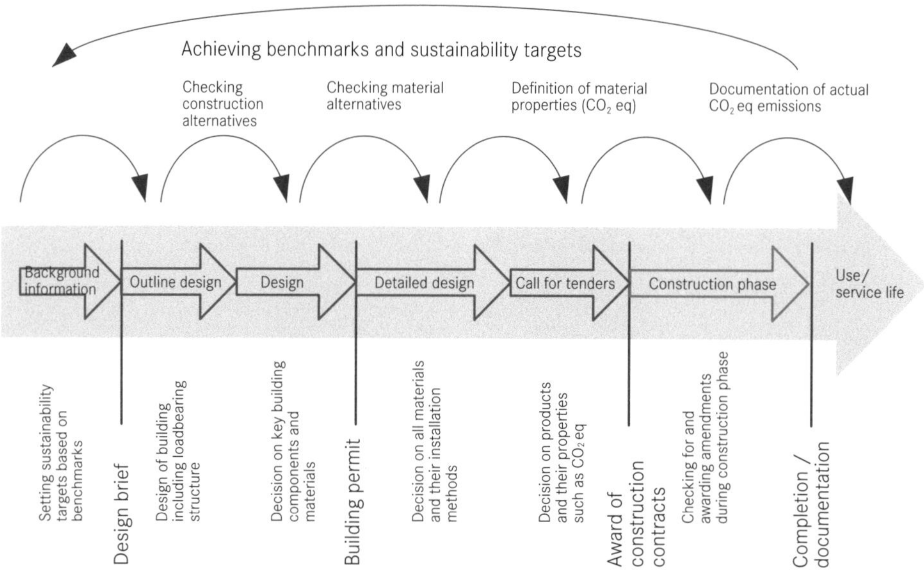

Fig. 54: Readjustments in the design process to reach CO_2 emission targets

CO_2 calculation underpinning design

As the design of a building becomes increasingly detailed, decisions are made regarding the choice of construction method and materials. As the design proceeds, it is normal practice to consider the cost of construction; it is equally as important to continue the calculation of CO_2 emissions. This makes it possible to made decisions not only with a view to esthetic and construction criteria, but also with respect to reducing CO_2 emissions. In this way targets that are set in the context of external framework conditions and/or building laws or client requirements can be achieved. Should deviations occur, it is always possible to carry out readjustments > Fig. 54.

BIM implementation

The building information modeling (BIM) method allows CO_2 emission values to be assigned directly to building components or materials.

■ **Tip**: The format used as the data interface in BIM models is Industry Foundation Classes (IFC), which can be used to exchange models within programs, including all attached information. This allows architects and planners to compare architectural and engineering models and to use current background data directly without having to manually compute or update quantities.

This makes it possible to estimate the effect of actions, such as the replacement of a material. In addition, there is the option, using additional software, to use the IFC files of the BIM model to carry out further sustainability simulations on the basis of the BIM model. ■

CONSTRUCTION PROCESS

Even though the essential decisions are made during the design process, it is possible - with appropriate preparation of the construction process - to implement additional criteria relating to sustainability and low CO_2 emissions. This affects the contractual arrangements with the building contractors and the actual performance of the construction work on site.

Definition of construction targets

If the CO_2 calculation has been continued throughout the design process, the respective consumption will have been established for all building materials and constructions. In order to ensure that these targets are actually met, it is necessary to agree them with the construction contractors. This means that the actual materials have to be listed in the specification or, if the specification is product-neutral, maximum CO_2 equivalents are listed. Likewise, the contract should contain arrangements about how waste and material offcuts are dealt with.

This puts the onus on the building contractors to document compliance with the contracted limit values using the quality seals or the EPD declarations of the manufacturers.

Resource consumption on the construction site

During the construction phase, building site waste presents an enormous problem. Work with reinforced concrete, and in situ concrete in particular, results in large amounts of waste from shuttering, props, reinforcement offcuts, and excess concrete. Use of partially prefabricated elements or components can help to reduce this waste significantly.

Irrespective of construction site waste management, most important decisions are made during the design process. For example, if the design includes facade grids that do not coincide with the sizes in which the concrete slabs are supplied, significant offcut waste of newly produced building material is created that has to be recycled.

Zero waste

The objective of specified values for the implementation on the construction site should be to produce as little waste as possible and to plan the use of materials in such a way that offcuts, the use of auxiliary

○ **Note**: Partially prefabricated elements consist of few-centimeter-thick concrete slabs that are accurately cast on a permanently used steel formwork. These slabs are then installed on site and set with concrete. Because they are mass produced in a factory, much less waste material is generated compared to on-site concrete work.

Fig. 55: Photos of construction site waste

materials, and energy use are minimized on the construction site. This approach, known as "zero waste", plays an important role not only during the construction phase but also during the service life and at the end of the building's lifecycle.

CONSIDERATION OF THE USE PHASE

In order to ensure the smooth operation of a building, the needs and demands associated with the use phase have to be taken into account even in the design process. Here it is particularly important that building components are easy to maintain and reach. If this is not taken into account during the design phase, it is likely that the building fabric would need to be modified during the use phase. ●

Facility management

Architects should provide appropriate access to all construction elements and installations and ensure that these can be easily maintained and cleaned. Larger clients often have a professional facility management team that deals with the operation and maintenance of the building. Here it is possible to apply the criteria of the future operation to the design of the building and components.

Use

As soon as a building is occupied, various maintenance, renovation, and conversion cycles must be taken into account. Many mechanically

● **Example**: Smoke detectors in suspended ceilings must be regularly checked for functionality. For this reason, it is necessary to use access flaps in the ceiling to ensure that they are easily accessible. If the gap above the suspended ceiling is small, a small flap directly beneath the smoke detector is sufficient. If it is necessary for a person to partially access the void above the ceiling to reach the smoke detector, this flap should measure at least 60 x 60 cm.

or electrically controlled components need regular maintenance in order to ensure long-term functionality. ○

When components reach the end of their lifecycle, they have to be replaced or repaired. This phase should also be taken into consideration during the design; for example, it should be possible to replace ventilation equipment via appropriate openings or to replace luminaires from high places within the building.

Conversion

If it is no longer possible to carry out the intended use on the basis of the original design, it becomes necessary to make modifications to the building components, the installations, or the building layout. In order to keep the obstacles as small as possible, the design of the building construction and the installations should consider these future needs. > Chapter Approaches to the Design Process

Conversion phases may involve only minor adaptations, or in the case of a complete redesign, the scope of a new building. When changes are forced owing to the presence of contaminants or because installations have to be renewed and sound building fabric has to be destroyed, this creates obstacles, high CO_2 emissions, and high costs. ●

Demolition

Buildings should not be demolished unless it is no longer possible to establish new use cycles through repair and conversion. In practice, however, there are many other reasons that determine this action. ○

The more the lifecycle of buildings is considered within the context of an optimized circular economy, the more environmentally friendly and climate-smart construction will become. Two key parameters for the future consumption of resources are that a) the design and implementation of construction measures take the environment and climate into account and that b) architects and clients focus on what already exists.

○ **Note**: Typical components include doors, windows, solar screening, heat generators, ventilation systems, risk sensors, detectors, wastewater processing, kitchen and services installations, as well as elevators. In many countries, maintenance cycles are regulated by law for safety reasons. However, for the purpose of ensuring long-term functionality, maintenance may need to be carried out much more frequently.

● **Example**: If, in an office building, data cables are installed under plaster or under the screed without revision openings, these parts have to be destroyed when these cables are replaced. If, on the other hand, cables are installed in conduits, ducts, data boxes, or dado trunking, they can be replaced without causing damage.

○ **Note**: Often buildings are demolished because the risks posed by the existing building appear greater at first sight than they actually are, a new building would allow the site to be more optimally used, the floor plan layout no longer meets current requirements, or the decision-makers simply no longer consider the architectural language appropriate for the time. In this case, the architects should first demonstrate solutions and options for using the existing building.

Summary

This volume covers a number of issues and criteria without being able to go into greater detail because of the limited scope of this book. We hope that readers are inspired to implement their own preferences and have been given ideas for the many ways in which we can handle the enormous climate change challenges faced by the construction industry in a creative manner. There is not one correct solution to any problem, but instead a mix of methods and strategies that must be checked for feasibility within a given project. The overarching aim must be to act in a resource-friendly and climate-smart manner, also at a small scale, which requires the will to embrace change and sometimes also to leave the well-trodden path in order to try or develop new approaches.

We are only at the beginning of a paradigm shift that will be forced upon us as global temperatures continue to rise. Like no previous era, this will impact design and construction with respect to esthetics, the value of existing buildings, construction methods, materials, and architectural outlook. There will be many new innovations and many changing requirements for clients and the design professions. We must actively engage in this process in order to achieve tangible changes towards a decarbonized world. This change will not be forced by big decisions made at UN climate conferences or through legislation. Rather, every one of us must play a role in this change and inspire and motivate others to do likewise.

Thus, this book should be understood as an overview aimed at arousing interest and encouraging readers to focus more deeply on various aspects of climate-smart design and construction and to incorporate these in their own work.

Appendices

REFERENCES

General literature on climate change

UN climate reports of the *Intergovernmental Panel on Climate Change* (IPCC)

Club of Rome (Ed.): *Earth for All: A Survival Guide for Our Planet*, oekom publishers, 2022

Sommer, B./Welzer, H.: *Transformation Design: A Social-Ecological Perspective;* in: Jonas, W./ Zerwas, S./von Anshelm, K. (Eds.): Transformation Design – Perspectives on a New Design Attitude; Board of International Research in Design, Birkhäuser, 2015.

Literature on design and construction

Cardelus Vidal, C.: *A Second Life for Buildings*, monsa, 2022

Röhlen, U./Ziegert, C.: *Earth Building Practice, Planning · Design · Building*, Beuth publishers, 2011

El khouli, S./John, V./Zeumer, M.: *Sustainable Construction Techniques*, Detail Greenbooks, 2014

Hebel, D./Wappner, L. et al.: *Building Sorted by Type: Methods, Materials, Constructions*, Edition Detail, 2024

Heisel, F./Hebel, D.: *Building Better – Less – Different: Circular Construction and Circular Economy: Fundamentals, Case Studies, Strategies,* Birkhäuser, 2022

Heisel, F./Hebel, D.: *Building Better – Less – Different: Clean Energy Transition and Digital Transformation,* Birkhäuser, 2023

Hillebrandt, A./Riegler-Floors, P./Rosen, A./Seggewies, J.-K.: *Atlas Recycling*, Edition Detail, 2021

Hofmeister, Sandra (Ed.): *Holzbauten/Timber Buildings*, Edition Detail, 2022

Kaufmann, H./Krötsch, S./Winter, S.: *Manual of Multistory Timber Construction*, Birkhäuser 2017

Ludwig, F./Schönle, D.: *Growing Architecture*, Birkhäuser, 2023

Minke, G./Krick, B.: *Straw Bale Construction Manual*, ökobuch, 2014

Nagler, F. (Ed.): *Building Simply – A Guideline*, Birkhäuser, 2022

Sobek, W.: *non nobis – On Building in the Future*, avedition, 2022

Steiger, L.: *Basics Timber Construction*, Birkhäuser, 2021

Watson, J.: Lo-TEK, *Design by Radical Indigenism*, Taschen, 2020

ZHAW (Ed.): *Re-use in Construction*, Park books, 2021

SOURCE REFERENCES FOR FIGURES

Fig. 1: Data sources: Climate College (2016): Historical greenhouse gas concentrations for climate modelling (CMIP6), Met Office (2022): HadCrut4 Data. www.metoffice.gov.uk, NOAA (2022): Trends in Atmospheric Carbon Dioxide. www.gml.noaa.gov

Fig. 2: Data source: IPCC Climate Change report 2014

Fig. 3: Following: Federal Ministry for Economic Affairs and Climate Action (BMWK) 2022 *Klimaschutz in Zahlen*, Fig. 7

Fig. 4: Data source: EEA, European Commission

Fig. 5: Data source: IPCC Climate Change report 2014

Fig. 6: Data source: IPCC Climate Change report 2014

Fig. 7: Following Will Steffen 2015/Linn Persson 2022/Wang-Erlandsson 2022

Fig. 8: Source: UN, United Nations Department of Global Communications

Fig. 9: Following Kate Raworth, *Doughnut Economics*, 2018

Fig. 10: Data source: IPCC Climate Change report 2014

Fig. 11: Data source DGNB 2021, *Benchmarks for Greenhouse Gas Emissions from Building Construction*

Fig. 12: Data source: cumulative EPD data from various manufacturers

Fig. 13: Data source: German Federal Environmental Agency

Fig. 14: Data source: BMWK, *Energiedaten: Gesamtausgabe* 2022

Fig. 15: Following Kalusche, Wolfdietrich: *Kostenplanung beim Altbau*, In: Deutsches Architektenblatt, 05/2007, pages 64 to 66

Fig. 17: Data source: Zimmermann/Reiser 2020

Fig. 18: Data source: Our World in Data/Statistical Review of World Energy & Ember

Fig. 19: Data source: Greenpeace

Fig. 32: Data source: BNB

Fig. 33: Following BNB, *Service Life of Building Components*

Fig. 37: Data source: ÖKOBAUDAT

Fig. 39: Data source: Federal Statistics Office (destatis) 2023

Fig. 40: Data source: Kreislaufwirtschaft Bau 2023

Fig. 42: Photo left: "Paulownia" by Jan Alonso under license CC BY-SA 2.0 DEED via Flickr

Fig. 43: Photo left "Straw Bale Wall Construction" by Chris RubberDragon under license CC BY-SA 2.0 DEED via Flickr; photo center "detail of the structure" by Nicolás Boullosa under license CC BY 2.0 DEED via Flickr; photo right by Nicolás Boullosa from Paris, France – plane tree cube is a solid steel structure covered by a skin of living plane tree branches, CC BY 2.0 via Wikipedia

Fig. 45: Photo left "Carrer Consell" by Cataleirxs under license CC BY-SA 4.0 DEED via Wikimedia

Fig. 46: Photo left “Pop-up-Bikelaine” by Onnola under license CC BY-SA 2.0 DEED via Flickr; photo right by Toniher under license CC BY-SA 3.0 DEED via Wikimedia
Fig. 47: Björn Vierhaus
Fig. 51: Students of Siegen University, winter semester 2023, the Urban Mining elective module
Fig. 56: Photo left “Concrete Waste” by Santeri Viinamäki under license CC BY-SA 4.0 DEED via Wikimedia

Special thanks to Katharina Schreider and Jana Steuer for their help in compiling the figures.

ABOUT THE AUTHOR

Prof. Dr.-Ing. Bert Bielefeld teaches architecture at the Neue Architekturschule Siegen (NAS) at the University of Siegen, Germany. He is also a managing partner with bertbielefeld&partner architekten in Dortmund.

Series editor: Bert Bielefeld
Conception: Bert Bielefeld, Annette Gref
Layout and cover design: Andreas Hidber
Translation into English: Hartwin Busch
English copy editing: Stephen Roche
Project management: Regina Herr
Production: Amelie Solbrig
Typesetting: Sven Schrape, Berlin

Paper: Magno Natural, 120 g/m^2
Printing: Beltz Grafische Betriebe

Library of Congress Control Number:
2024934502

Bibliographic information published by the German National Library
The German National Library lists this publication in the Deutsche Nationalbibliografie; detailed bibliographic data are available on the Internet at http://dnb.dnb.de.

ISBN 978-3-0356-2756-5

e-ISBN (PDF) 978-3-0356-2757-2
German Print ISBN 978-3-0356-2755-8

Im Westfeld 8, 4055 Basel, Switzerland
Part of Walter de Gruyter GmbH, Berlin/Boston

FSC www.fsc.org MIX Papier | Fördert gute Waldnutzung FSC® C089473

9 8 7 6 5 4 3 2 1
www.birkhauser.com